A Friedman Lecture Fund Monograph

W0017369

THE SCHEME OF CONTROL
ON ELECTRICITY COMPANIES

The Hong Kong Centre for Economic Research

The Centre was set up as a research and educational trust under a trust deed signed in 1987. It supports research and publishes studies on public policy issues to promote understanding of economic affairs and provide alternative policy choices.

The Centre's work is assisted by an international board of advisers:

The Centre is an approved tax-exempted charitable trust controlled by Trustees and financed by sales of publications and voluntary contributions from individuals, organizations and companies.

Prof. Y. C. Richard Wong, Director

The Hong Kong Centre for Economic Research
School of Economics and Finance
The University of Hong Kong
Pokfulam Road, Hong Kong
Tel: (852) 2547 8313   Fax: (852) 2548 6319

A Friedman Lecture Fund Monograph

The Scheme of Control on Electricity Companies

Pun-lee LAM

Published for

The Hong Kong Centre for Economic Research

by

The Chinese University Press

ISBN 962–201–754–1

THE CHINESE UNIVERSITY PRESS
The Chinese University of Hong Kong
SHA TIN, N. T., HONG KONG

Fax: (852) 2603 6692
E-mail: cup@cuhk.edu.hk
Web-site: http://www.cuhk.edu.hk/cupress/w1.htm

Printed in Hong Kong

The Friedman Lecture Fund

The Friedman Lecture Fund was established from proceeds obtained from a public lecture given by Dr. Milton Friedman on 24 September 1988 in Hong Kong. The purpose of the Fund is to support research that leads to an improved understanding of the role of markets in economic life. To this end the Fund supports the work of individual scholars and institutions. The Fund is operated jointly by the Hong Kong Centre for Economic Research and the School of Economics and Finance of The University of Hong Kong.

Contents

List of Illustrations

Foreword

The HKCER Paperbacks are planned to be studies of medium length in which economists would analyze policy issues from an economic perspective. Authors are invited, in particular, to consider the circumstances which encouraged or inhibited the translation of ideas into policy.

The power industry in Hong Kong has been regulated under a unique Scheme of Control that is different from the rate-of-return regulation model in the United States and the price-cap approach to regulation in the United Kingdom. Dr. Pun-lce Lam explains in this pioneering study the detailed regulatory mechanisms of the Hong Kong scheme and its implications for economic efficiency and consumer interests. He also considers various measures that can improve the regulatory mechanisms as well as measures to enhance competition in the supply of electricity.

He shows how the Hong Kong Scheme of Control, which provides for a development fund to stabilize returns and finance expansion, has advantages not possessed by the U.S. and U.K. regulatory structures and helps to enhance productive efficiency of the firm. Nevertheless, he finds that the interests of the regulated companies are protected by the Scheme of Control, often at the expense of consumer interests.

He identifies areas where the scheme is deficient and can be improved upon. His study finds that permitting differential rates of return for equity and debt financed expansion is an undesirable feature of the scheme and the failure to take into account the effects on inflation on the rate of return is also an important problem given Hong Kong's high inflation rate in recent years. He is particularly critical of the high net rate of return permitted on expansion financed by the development fund. This last feature allows the company to earn a rate of return on equity that is substantially above

that permitted by the Scheme of Control without benefiting customers.

Different issues on regulation and competition in supplying
electricity are also considered in the study. For example, whether
electricity companies should be allowed to diversify into other lines
of business, whether the companies should be mandated to share their
transmission and distribution networks upon payment of an access fee
to enhance competition, whether future demand for electricity should
be met by importing surplus electricity from China or through building new power generating facilities.

This is a highly useful study of one important aspect of Hong
Kong's power industry which has come under increasing public
scrutiny and review. Government attempts to regulate the industry
should not ignore the obvious gains that can be obtained by relying on
other changes that would enhance market mechanisms in the power
industry.

The Trustees, Advisers and Director of the Hong Kong Centre for
Economic Research must formally dissociate themselves from the
conclusions of the Paperback, while welcoming its timely contribu-
tion to a major issue in Hong Kong.

Y. C. Richard Wong
May 1996

Executive Summary

In Hong Kong, electricity is supplied by two private companies: China Light and Power Company Limited (CLP) and Hongkong Electric Company Limited (HEC). These two companies are subject to a special regulatory arrangement called the Scheme of Control. The Scheme, which was proposed by the industry itself, is essentially a long-term regulatory contract between a private firm and the Hong Kong Government. Under the Scheme of Control, a regulated utility is subject to both (nominal) rate-of-return control and price control.

In Hong Kong, the Scheme of Control has often been equated to rate-of-return regulation in the United States, and effects of the Scheme of Control have been analyzed within the framework of traditional regulatory constraint on the behaviour of a regulated firm. These types of analyses have failed to consider the major differences between the two systems and therefore their conclusions have been drawn from the U.S. system instead of from the Scheme of Control. In this study, we try to examine the regulatory effects of the Scheme and suggest a tentative approach to restructuring the electricity industry in Hong Kong based on experiences in the United States and the United Kingdom.

The major findings of our study are:

1. The Scheme of Control in Hong Kong is a formal long-term contract between a private firm and the Government. The Scheme allows a regulated firm to enjoy certain permitted returns, in return for promised levels of services. The regulatory contract period is fixed at 15 years, which provides enough protection for regulated firms to earn sufficient returns to recover their sunk investment costs. Over the past three decades, the Scheme has achieved its objective of providing an adequate incentive for the two electricity

companies to expand capacity in order to meet the demands for electricity in Hong Kong.

2. The regulatory process in Hong Kong is entirely different from the rate-of-return regulation in the United States. Governance costs are lower under the Hong Kong system, but there is also less transparency. In addition, the price adjustment mechanism is unlike the price-cap regulation in the United Kingdom. Prices charged by utilities under the Scheme are not capped. The two regulated electricity companies institute price decreases only when their development funds and rate reduction reserves exceed certain limits.

3. Most rate-of-return regulation models assume a single allowed rate of return without considering the effects of differential allowed rates for equity and debt capital. The effects of rate-of-return regulation are analyzed under the simple Averch-Johnson framework. Our analysis suggests that with differential permitted rates of return, there would be significant effects on the capital structure as well as on the input choice. When the permitted rate of return on debt capital exceeds the debt cost, a regulated firm will tend to over-expand and rely on its debt capital. By debt financing, the two electricity companies can actually earn rates of return of more than 20% on equity, which far exceeds the permitted rate of return on equity set at 15%.

4. It has been found that a higher debt-equity ratio does not raise the financial risk of a regulated firm under the Scheme of Control. This is because the firm is protected by a long-term regulatory contract, and because the development fund can help stabilize earnings. CLP argues that the Scheme of Control can facilitate low cost debt financing. But has the company shared the benefits with its customers?

5. The conventional wisdom is that even if the regulator sets the permitted rate of return at a level equal to the cost of capital, the regulated firm will be indifferent between all feasible input combinations that meet the regulatory constraint because they all involve zero profit. The regulated firm will not

have an incentive to choose the input combination which minimizes costs. However, if profits or excess earnings are to be transferred to a development fund (which may be drawn from later when the company is in an unfavourable state), then the regulated firm will have some incentive to attain (*ex-post*) productive efficiency. However, the firm tends to over-report costs (and revenue requirements) so as to accumulate the development fund (for financing expansion and stabilizing returns).

6. When the permitted rate of return on development fund capital is higher than its interest cost, there will be a different incentive for a regulated firm to accumulate the development fund. By overcharging, the regulated firm is able to borrow money from its customers at a relatively low interest cost.

7. Direct comparison of electricity prices in Hong Kong with those in other countries is not useful because electricity companies in other countries operate under different economic and regulatory environments. Population density and government taxes (or subsidies) also have a direct effect on electricity prices.

8. Because the expected useful lives of fixed assets have been set too low, electricity users have paid higher prices due to the early retirement of the two companies' generating facilities. Users have also paid more because the actual rate of return on equity capital is higher than the cost of equity capital, and because of CLP's expansion to meet demand from China in the 1980s. Furthermore, electricity prices in Hong Kong have fluctuated widely. The construction of coal-fired generators increased prices sharply in the early 1980s, but once the generators had been commissioned, the two electricity companies were able to lower their prices due to the decrease in fuel cost. Wide fluctuations in electricity prices in Hong Kong are the result of electric utilities being able to raise prices whenever costs increase. Significant increases in electricity prices are expected in the next few years

if the Government does not revise the terms of the existing Schemes.

9. HEC has been charging prices (5% to 20%) higher than CLP; this may be due to the difference in the scale of production or the difference in the efficiency of its operations. Attempts should be made to eliminate this tariff differential. In addition, a system with permitted returns based on asset value would not encourage the two companies to adopt genuine demand-side management or energy conservation.

10. As compared to the beta values in U.K. and U.S. utilities, firms under the Scheme of Control in Hong Kong have higher beta values (and higher costs of capital). This can be partly explained by the fact that some regulated utilities in Hong Kong have been involved in riskier non-regulated businesses, which would raise the beta values of their stocks. The main reason for higher beta values, however, is the regulatory system itself. Since the Scheme of Control regulates nominal returns rather than real returns, the real returns of regulated utilities are greatly affected by inflation. As the inflation rate in Hong Kong rises and varies over time, the real returns earned by these regulated utilities also fluctuate.

Our findings have shown that the Scheme of Control has served to protect the interests of the two electricity companies. While consumers have enjoyed adequate electricity supply and reasonable tariffs, the tariffs could be lower if some of the terms in the Scheme were refined. As did previous Schemes, the new Scheme of Control agreements (scheduled to be in effect until 2008) contain a five year review clause. Either party, the Government or the regulated electric utility can ask for a revision of terms of the agreement. Such a request should be made before the end of the company's financial year in 1998. Hence, despite the fact that both companies are now operating under the new Scheme of Control, the Hong Kong Government can still initiate changes under the terms of the Scheme. In view of the recent changes in the operating environment of the energy industry, we make the following recommendations to improve the existing Scheme of Control:

1. In order to measure the cost of capital more precisely, regulated electricity companies should not be allowed to diversify. Such structural separation can also help prevent cost-shifting and cross-subsidization.

2. Given that the Scheme of Control is to be retained, some interim reviews on tariffs and permitted returns are needed. A system of graduated permitted rates of return could help stabilize prices over time. Price-cap constraints could be incorporated into the Scheme so as to encourage efficient production.

3. The development fund arrangement should be retained. Apart from its dual function of financing system expansion and stabilizing returns, the fund provides an incentive for a regulated firm to achieve productive efficiency. However, the permitted rate of return imposed on capital financed by the development fund should be closer to actual interest rates.

4. Permitted rates of return should not be based simply on assets. The permitted rates of return should be set at levels which correctly reflect the equity cost, debt cost, and inflation rate. Finance theories should be applied in determining the permitted rates of return.

5. Self-revelation mechanisms should be introduced in the regulatory process to induce truthful revelation of cost and demand forecasts.

6. In the long term, competition should be introduced into the energy market. Regulated electricity companies should be mandated to share their transmission and distribution networks upon payment of an access fee.

7. Competition in the generation and supply of electricity, particularly at the wholesale level, should be encouraged. Import of surplus electricity from China should also be supported. Increased competition would lower costs and

close the tariff differential between CLP and HEC. Competition would also encourage demand-side management to lower costs and tariffs.

8. Electricity companies should not be allowed to build new generating facilities unless the full avoided cost (incremental cost) of electricity is lower than the purchase price charged by generators in other areas. They should be allowed to share the benefit of the cost avoided because of their effort to promote energy conservation.

9. Because of the slowing down of demand growth for electricity, CLP should reconsider its construction plan of gas-fired generators. In addition, if importing electricity would be cheaper, then some of these generating facilities would not be necessary. The natural gas saved from generating electricity could be used for other purposes, such as for cooking and heating.

10. As the electricity system in Hong Kong expands and integrates with the system in southern China, the Government should consider whether it is necessary to set up a unified regulatory body governing the electricity industry. The role of this regulatory body, if created, should be restricted to formulating coherent policies to enhance efficiency and market competition in the electricity industry.

Acknowledgements

I would like to thank Professor Paul Grout, supervisor during my Ph.D. dissertation, for his continuing encouragement, support and careful advice. He has shared with me his extensive knowledge in the field of government regulation of public utilities and has provided me with invaluable suggestions during the past few years.

I would like to express my gratitude to two anonymous referees for their generous and enlightening comments and advice. This has enabled me to improve and expand my knowledge of the field enormously. Throughout my study, I received kind support from the electricity and gas companies in Hong Kong. They generously provided me with the requested information and made every effort to check their company records and documents.

Pun-lee Lam

The Author

Dr. Pun-lee Lam received his Ph.D. degree in Economics from the University of Bristol in 1995. He is currently working as an assistant professor at the Hong Kong Polytechnic University. Dr. Lam's research interest is the study of government regulation of public utilities. His Ph.D. dissertation was written on the government control of electricity companies and his research results have been published in numerous local and international journals and magazines.

CHAPTER 1

Introduction

Electricity industries in most countries have been subject to various forms of government control either for economic or political reasons. Electric power companies in the United States are subject to the rate-of-return regulation. They are regulated by commissions with extensive authority to inquire into all aspects of a utility's operations. In the United Kingdom, the firms in the electricity supply industry (ESI) were, until recently, under public ownership and control. Most of these firms were privatized in 1990 and are now subject to the price-cap regulation. In Hong Kong, the two electricity companies are subject to a special regulatory arrangement called the Scheme of Control. The Scheme, which was proposed by the industry itself, is essentially a long-term regulatory contract between a private firm and the Hong Kong Government. Under the Scheme of Control, a regulated utility is subject to both (nominal) rate-of-return control and price control.

In addition to the two regional monopolists in electricity supply, two franchised bus companies and one telephone company in Hong Kong have also been subject to a similar Scheme of Control. In Hong Kong, the Scheme of Control has often been equated to the rate-of-return regulation in the United States, and effects of the Scheme of Control have been analyzed within the framework of traditional regulatory constraint on the behaviour of a regulated firm. These types of analyses, however, have failed to consider the major differences between the two systems and therefore their conclusions have been drawn from the U.S. system instead of from the Scheme of Control.

Over the past decade, electricity industries in many countries have undergone substantial change in their organizational structure. In some cases the electric utilities were privatized, while in others, competition replaced monopoly in certain stages of the industry. Despite this current of competition, the structure of the electricity industry in Hong Kong remains the same as it was thirty years ago. The industry is still monopolized by two private firms without any direct or indirect competition between them. In this study, we try to learn from the lessons provided by the United States and the United Kingdom, and suggest a tentative approach to restructuring the electricity industry in Hong Kong.

This book is organized in the following way: in Chapter 2 we provide a background to the electricity industry in Hong Kong with a focus on the events which led to the imposition of the Scheme of Control on CLP and outline some of the special features of the scheme. In Chapter 3 we describe the regulatory environments of the electricity industry in the United States and the United Kingdom. We compare the Scheme of Control with the regulatory systems in these two countries. In Chapter 4 the Scheme of Control mechanism is fully explained. The effects of the Scheme on the capital structure, input choice and productive efficiency within a regulated firm are also evaluated. Chapters 5 and 6 are devoted to discussing the empirical results on the performance of the two electricity companies. Based on our empirical studies and the experience in other countries, we provide our conclusions and recommendations in Chapter 7.

CHAPTER 2

The Electricity Industry in Hong Kong

At present, electricity is provided by two commercial companies. The Hongkong Electric Company Limited (HEC) supplies electricity to Hong Kong Island and the neighbouring islands of Ap Lei Chau and Lamma, while China Light and Power Company Limited (CLP) serves the whole of Kowloon and the New Territories, including Lantau and a number of outlying islands. Both companies are listed on the Hong Kong Stock Exchange and neither operate on a franchise basis. However, the Hong Kong Government monitors the two companies through the Scheme of Control. In this chapter, we provide a background to the electricity industry in Hong Kong and discuss the events which led to the imposition of the Scheme of Control, as well as highlighting special features of the scheme.

2.1 The Electricity Industry in Hong Kong

(1) Before the 1950s

Both electricity companies have a long history in Hong Kong. HEC was the first electricity company in Hong Kong. It was incorporated in 1889 and began supplying electricity to Hong Kong Island in December 1890. CLP was incorporated in Hong Kong in 1901 for the purpose of supplying electricity to Canton (in China) and Kowloon (and later to the New Territories and many outlying islands). It was wound-up and incorporated again in 1918.

Until the early 1980s there was another smaller electricity company in Hong Kong called the Cheung Chau Electric Company Limited. This company was founded in 1913, originally as a community project, and supplied electricity to the population and industries on Cheung Chau Island. In January 1984, the Government authorized CLP to provide electricity to Cheung Chau. An agreement was reached between CLP and the Cheung Chau Electric Company by which CLP acquired the assets of the latter, thus allowing the islanders to benefit from the lower electricity tariffs which applied elsewhere in the New Territories. Historically, there were other minor enterprises, including village co-operatives, which produced electricity for remote localities. After the Second World War, CLP expanded its services to these areas and most of those co-operatives were closed. Therefore, electricity is currently supplied by two commercial regional monopolists: CLP and HEC.

(2) The Nationalization Fiasco of the 1960s[1]

CLP and HEC are investor-owned companies and until 1964, they were not subject to any government control except for safety aspects. However, in response to public resentment in the 1950s towards poor service and high tariffs, an Electricity Supply Companies Commission was appointed by the Government in July 1959, to investigate the workings of CLP and HEC.

Complaints about tariffs had been voiced as early as 1946, soon after the Second World War. At that time the Financial Secretary, after consultation with CLP, sent a letter to the Chairman of the complaining party, the Kowloon Merchants' Association. The letter stated that "There can be no question of Government instructing the China Light and Power Company to reduce their electricity rates. The Company is a private enterprise, and Government cannot interfere unless it considers that the Company is acting against public interest. The conduct of [the Company] has been consistently co-operative with Govern-

---

1. The information in this section is primarily based on two books (Coates 1977 and Cameron 1982) which describe the historical development of the two electricity companies in Hong Kong. Other information has been collected from the two companies' annual reports, the Hong Kong Government's annual reports and other published documents relating to the operations and regulations of the two companies.

ment policy and we are satisfied that as soon as it is economically possible for them to reduce their rates they will do so." (Cameron 1982, pp. 183–184).

By the end of 1948, however, the Government felt that some measure of control on tariffs and dividends was necessary. CLP sought the opinion of a British lawyer and he affirmed that as the company was registered as an ordinary company free from any statutory control, any control on its dividends would be a confiscation of the shareholders' interests. After an exchange of letters between CLP and the Government, the matter was dropped.

In 1952, CLP and HEC announced that a fuel surcharge of 17% would be imposed on all bills. The surcharge was lowered in the ensuing years. The purpose of imposing the fuel surcharge was to protect the two companies from unstable oil prices. In 1957, following the Suez Crisis, the surcharge was raised from 9% to 18%. The new surcharge was strongly opposed by industrialists. The dissatisfaction among large consumers was highlighted in a petition sent to the Governor by the Kowloon Chamber of Commerce. A committee of industrialists, mostly from Kowloon, was formed with the intent to oppose the increase. Another petition, led by the Chinese General Chamber of Commerce, asked for a commission of inquiry, demanded state control of the two companies and accused HEC of "destroying industry".[2] The Chairman of the Chinese Manufacturers' Union even pointed out that all modern cities had public utilities run by governments. The *Hong Kong Standard*, one of the few English newspapers in Hong Kong, carried a weighty editorial on 11 December 1958, with the headline, "More Power to You". Both companies were accused of charging high power rates and not informing the factories of power disruptions in the past two years.[3]

---

2. See Coates 1977, p. 186. The writer provided a historical background of the formation of the Commission in Chapter 21.

3. The editorial article suggested that there had been more than 3,354 minutes of power disruptions of supply to industries in the New Territories over the last two years. Manufacturers vowed that they had lost $15 for every minute without power, in overhead expenses alone.

The editorial article was followed on the next day by a letter from civic leaders and industrialists, arguing that from the "huge profits" of the company, a "special reserve fund" could easily be set aside to meet unexpected increases in fuel costs and freight. The writer favoured raising capital for modernizing the plants of the two companies and argued that the money should not come from consumers (Cameron 1982, p. 185). The later formation of a development fund under the Scheme of Control may have originated from this idea of setting up a special reserve fund from the company's huge profits to meet unexpected changes in costs.

Amid public outcry the Governor at that time, Sir Robert Black, appointed on 16 July 1959 a three-man commission called the Electricity Supply Companies Commission. Two of the Commission members were from England (one of whom was a former chairman of the regional boards of Britain's nationalized electricity supply) and the third was from Hong Kong. The Commission held a series of public hearings. The two companies were represented by their Chairmen: Lawrence Kadoorie of CLP and William Stoker of HEC. Numerous complaints and comments about the two companies were received, including outdated equipment, high tariffs and surcharges, stoppages without warnings and excessive profits.

During the hearings, it was revealed that it was the policy of CLP to "subsidize industry". This policy, it was stated, had been adopted in order to help and encourage industry and thereby increase employment. The tariff for bulk supply, enjoyed by industrial users, was fixed arbitrarily at a level which did not reflect the cost of the service. In some cases, the tariff was even below the cost of production (Hong Kong Government, Electricity Supply Companies Commission 1959, p. 15). As industrialists were the major beneficiaries from CLP's underpricing policy, it defied logic that they should continue to demand nationalized power. Perhaps they thought that this would be even better and cheaper, though the two companies warned that this would not be so if power was under the control of bureaucrats. CLP's underpricing policy was strongly criticized in the hearings, as it gave undue preference to one group of consumers (industrial users) against others (residential and commercial users).

The Commission submitted its report in December 1959. Instead of proposing any form of government regulation, the Commission recommended an outright takeover of the two companies by the Government, in order to "permanently remove the competing interest between the shareholders and the public". This result was not very surprising considering the Commission's composition and the prevailing climate in post-war Britain in favour of nationalizing all big companies, especially those in the field of public utilities. As expected, the recommendation received great resistance from the two companies. They asked the Government not to take any action until they had prepared and submitted alternative proposals of their own. This was agreed to by the Government (Hong Kong Government 1960, pp. 212–213).

As an interim measure to safeguard the assets of the two companies, the Government restricted the rate of dividends for the current and succeeding years to $1.1 per share, which was the rate that existed before the appointment of the Commission. CLP reacted by putting the excess dividends into two special reserve accounts known as the Dividend Adjustment Account and the Tariff Adjustment Account. These reserves were expected to be used for increasing dividends and reducing tariffs once the dividend restraint was removed. Perhaps the development fund, which was established later under the Scheme of Control, was a continuation of these two special reserve accounts. The dividend restraint was eventually relaxed in 1963.

Meanwhile, the Government was reluctant to pursue a policy of nationalization as this would have great financial implications. The two companies would be taken over by compulsory purchase, in the form of 6.5% interest stock with an ultimate redemption date of approximately 35 years from the date of issue. The amount allotted would be $220 million for CLP and $208 million for HEC. The directors of HEC considered the terms to be inadequate, arguing that the Government had the right to acquire the company, but only in cash. They stated that it was "inequitable to compel the shareholders to take a fixed interest stock in exchange for an equity in a rapidly expanding industry." (Coates 1977, p. 190)

Negotiations between the Government and the two companies continued, in an attempt to devise some form of public control different from the compulsory public acquisition recommended by the Commission. In his annual review, dated 24 November 1960, Kadoorie suggested that the British rather than the American tradition in electricity regulation should be followed, in order to secure simplicity in administration and to avoid undue interference. He proposed that dividends and profits should be retained for investment and be limited to a fixed sum per unit sold. For each unit sold, CLP would be entitled to a certain margin of profit, and within this margin, to a certain margin of dividend. Furthermore, dividends should be limited to a standard margin and the difference between this dividend margin and the standard margin of profit should be allowed for a standard margin of retention, which would broadly be in line with the needs of normal expansion (Coates 1977, p. 190).[4] The scheme aroused widespread disapproval and was rejected by the Government, who was still reluctant to take over the two companies.

In May 1962, a provisional agreement was made between the Government and the Boards of Directors of the two companies. The agreement covered the merger of the companies, and an arrangement for the linking of future increases in dividends with reductions in charges. However, in July 1962, the merger terms did not gain the consent from enough CLP shareholders. The Government proposed that the merger terms should be subject to an independent assessment. However, towards the end of the year, HEC announced that it could not accept this and it became increasingly clear that a voluntary merger was unlikely. The problem of the future control of the companies remained unsolved after three years of negotiations (Hong Kong Government 1962).

The Chairman of CLP, Lawrence Kadoorie, became very anxious about the future development of the company, as well as the future supply of electricity in Hong Kong. He felt that any further delay in

---

4. Also see CLP's annual report of 1960, pp. 13–14 and Cameron 1982, pp. 198–199.

reaching an agreement with the Government would cause an inadequate electricity supply in the coming years. He tried to break the
stalemate by finding a strong foreign business partner who could help
provide enough capital for system expansion. In November 1964,
CLP, in cooperation with Esso Eastern Inc. (the trade name for the
overseas operations of the parent company Exxon), proposed a
Scheme of Control for 15 years (lasting until September 1978) and
eventually reached an agreement with the Government.

The objectives of the Scheme were to limit the disposable profits
of the companies to a reasonable return on their equity capital while
providing adequate incentives towards efficiency and expansion. In
particular, it would ensure that the benefits from any capital for
expansion obtained from additional profits would go primarily to the
consumer.[5] CLP promised to reduce the tariffs and set limits on
dividends in subsequent years. These objectives were to be achieved
by setting up a development fund. Any excess profits would be put
into this fund and used for acquiring fixed assets. The interest accrued
would be used for reducing tariffs. It was agreed between CLP and the
Government that the fund would constitute a liability, not an asset, of
the company. Other important features of the joint-venture between
CLP and Esso included:

— The formation of a new generating company, the Peninsula
   Electric Power Company Limited (PEPCO), which was
   jointly owned by CLP (40 percent) and Esso (60 percent).
   The electricity generated was to be sold exclusively to CLP
   and distributed through CLP's system.
— Both CLP and PEPCO would, as soon as possible, purchase
   all their existing petroleum requirements at competitive
   prices from Esso under a long-term fuel supply contract.

The formation of PEPCO, in fact, was a way to get around the

---

5. The objectives and features of the proposed Scheme of Control were laid down
   in CLP's annual report of 1964.

Foreign Assets Control Regulations in the United States, which
prohibited transactions with communist China. Esso was not allowed
to acquire shares of CLP directly, as it might sell electricity to communist China. This agreement was a great surprise to the Shell Company of Hong Kong Limited, which had previously supplied fuel to
CLP. However, Shell continued to be the fuel supplier to HEC. Although HEC was not formally subject to the Scheme of Control until
1979 (when CLP renewed its contract with the Government), the
company maintained close cooperation with the Government on all
matters concerning tariff policy (HEC 1978, p. 7).

(3) Oil Shocks in the 1970s

In the 1970s, the cost of fuel oil constituted a large part of the running
costs of the two electricity companies, due to the fact that their
generating units mainly consumed fuel oil. In 1970, HEC entered into
a long-term contract with Shell for fuel oil. However, as fuel oil prices
were rising continuously, a disagreement arose between HEC and
Shell with regard to the correct interpretation, meaning, and effect of
certain provisions connected with prices in the new contract (HEC
1971). Shell demanded, under the terms of the new agreement, to
renegotiate the basic prices for fuel oil on the grounds that a major
dislocation of normal world oil supply patterns had taken place in
the early 1970s. HEC contended that Shell had no valid grounds on
which to make this demand. Consequently, HEC and Shell com-
menced legal proceedings in the Supreme Court of Hong Kong in
1972. In 1974, HEC entered a new agreement with Shell which,
among other things, provided for the annual revision of fuel prices
(HEC 1974).

In 1973 and 1974, the price of fuel oil rose sharply to about four
times its former level, bringing about a substantial increase in the fuel
cost adjustment portion of electricity tariffs. In addition, marked
increases in other costs caused an increase in basic tariff of one cent
per unit by CLP in April 1974. This was the first increase in many
years. Since fuel oil was in short supply, the Government had to
impose restrictions on the use of electricity during the first few

months of 1974. These restrictions were lifted towards the end of May once the supply situation improved.

In April 1979, owing to another fuel oil shortage, the Government decided to implement oil conservation measures. The Oil (Conservation and Control) Ordinance 1979 conferred upon the Governor in Council and the Director of Oil Suppliers to give directions to suppliers and dealers as to the storage, supply, use and disposal of oil and to give similar directions to electricity and gas companies (Hong Kong Government 1980, p. 147). A package of conservation measures was introduced in May 1979 but most parts were lifted by October 1979 when the oil supply situation improved. To lessen Hong Kong's dependence on oil and to help keep down costs for consumers, the two electricity companies decided to construct new generators which would be capable of being fired by coal or oil. As a result, the effects of the substantial increase in oil prices during the Gulf War of 1990–1991 had a limited effect on the prices charged by the two companies. In addition, in order to maintain security of supply, CLP and HEC's policy was to procure fuel from widely diversified sources (CLP 1990, HEC 1983).

(4) Rapid Expansion in the 1980s

During the 1970s, HEC diversified its activities to non-utility areas. In July 1976, HEC and other subsidiaries were grouped under an umbrella company, Hongkong Electric Holdings Limited. In April 1982, the Hongkong Land Company Limited acquired 34% of HEC's equity (HEC 1982). In January 1985, the debt-ridden Hongkong Land decided to sell its holding to Hutchison Whampoa in order to reduce its debt-equity ratio. Then in March 1987, the Board of Directors of HEC proposed a reorganization in order to separate utility and non-utility activities. This reorganization was approved and became effective in June 1987.

For CLP, there were no major structural changes in the company despite the fact that it had been expanding at even faster rate than HEC in the last few decades (see Figure 2.1), particularly during the 1980s. In the early 1960s, CLP had already launched a subsidized

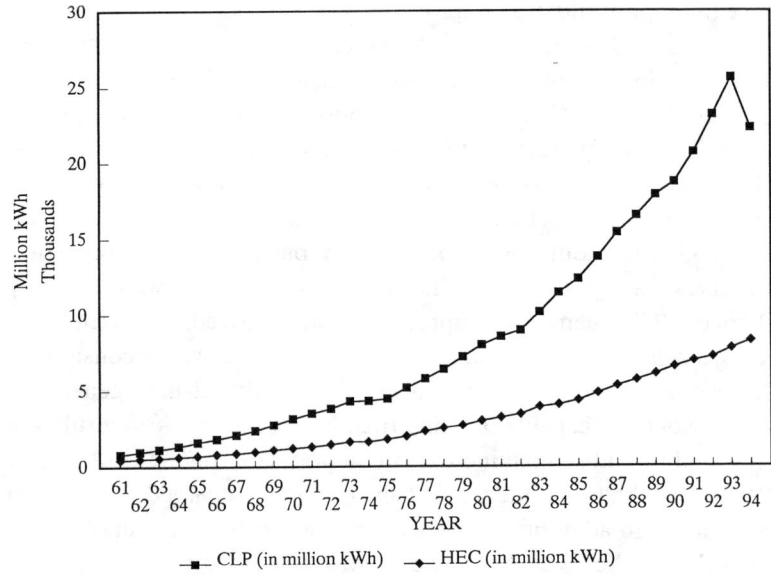

Figure 2.1   Electricity Supply in Hong Kong

____ CLP (in million kWh)   ___ HEC (in million kWh)

Sources: Annual reports of CLP and HEC, 1961–1994.

electrification scheme. Under this scheme, more and more villages in the remote areas were connected to the company's supply system, no matter how small the village was or how unprofitable it was to do so. Apart from the formation of PEPCO in 1964, two additional associated generating companies, Kowloon Electricity Supply Company Limited (KESCO) and Castle Peak Power Company Limited (CAPCO), were formed in 1978 and 1981, respectively. The shares of these two companies, similar to the previous arrangement, are held 40% by CLP and 60% by Exxon Energy Limited (a wholly owned subsidiary of Esso Eastern Inc.).

Lawrence Kadoorie, Chairman of CLP from 1956 to 1993, envisaged expanding the company's supply area to mainland China. This began to materialize in the 1980s.

The question of supplying electricity to Guangdong Province of the People's Republic of China was first raised when Kadoorie visited Beijing in May 1978 (CLP 1979). A series of meetings between CLP and Guangdong Power Company (renamed Guangdong General Power Company GGPC in 1984) later took place. The outcome was an agreement to interconnect the systems of the two companies and for CLP to supply electricity to Guangdong at a bulk tariff rate. However, Guangdong's reliance on CLP's supply of electricity decreased in recent years. In 1986, CLP reached a coal/electricity agreement with GGPC to solve the latter's insufficient foreign exchange problem. Under the agreement, GGPC would pay for part of its electricity purchases by means of delivery of coal to CLP, which in turn would resell the coal to its associated generating companies (CLP 1986).

From discussions on the interconnection between CLP and Guangdong Power Company, the question of constructing a nuclear power station in Guangdong to supply electricity to Guangdong and Hong Kong was raised (CLP 1980). A joint study of the viability of such a project was conducted by the two companies. CLP invited experts from the Central Electricity Generating Board and the Atomic Energy Authority of the United Kingdom to participate in the study. The study was completed in late 1980; the report concluded that it was technically feasible to erect a nuclear power station with two 900 MW pressurized water reactors in southern Guangdong Province. CLP realized that the building of a nuclear power station was beyond the financial capability of the company. This, coupled with political implications and the ramifications of entering into the nuclear power field (such as fuel procurement, storage and disposal), made it clear that the project could only be implemented on a government to government basis.

During 1982, supplementary studies were carried out and meetings were held between representatives of the British and Chinese Governments (CLP 1982). In late 1982, the Chinese Government completed its review of the feasibility study and announced its decision to proceed with the development of the nuclear power station at Daya Bay (CLP 1983). Following that decision, the Hong Kong Government appointed Lazard Brothers & Company Limited to examine the economic aspects of the project. In early November 1983, the Hong Kong Government announced its willingness for Hong Kong to purchase electricity generated by the nuclear power station.

The building of a nuclear power station at Daya Bay proceeded. The station is now operated by the Guangdong Nuclear Power Joint Venture Company (GNPJVC), in which the Guangdong Nuclear Investment Company (GNIC) holds a 75% interest and the Hong Kong Nuclear Investment Company (HKNIC) (wholly owned by CLP), holds a 25% interest. The two companies signed the joint-venture contract on 18 January 1985. The first unit of the Daya Bay Station was planned to start operating in 1992 and the second unit about a year later. It was anticipated that about 70% of the power from this station would be supplied to Hong Kong. In spite of great opposition from the Hong Kong public, the Government decided to proceed with the project. After some delays, the Daya Bay nuclear power station started operating in mid-1993.

Since 1983, CLP has signed other agreements with China. In 1985, the company signed an agreement with the China Merchants Steam Navigation Company Limited (CMSN) for a ten year supply of electricity to the Shekou Industrial Zone and the adjacent Che Wan area, both in Guangdong Province (CLP 1986). In December 1990, CLP, through its associate, Hong Kong Pumped Storage Development Company Limited (PSDC), reached an agreement for the right to use 50% of the pumped storage power station (capacity 1,200 MW), which was constructed at Conghua, north of Guangzhou. PSDC's shares are divided between Exxon Energy Limited (51%) and CLP (49%). Since the project is outside Hong Kong, the investment is not governed by the Scheme of Control (CLP 1991). Furthermore, CLP has also maintained close links with other power companies in China through various feasibility studies and training courses.

At present, CLP's system is interconnected with that of HEC. Initially, the interconnection commissioned in 1981 had a capacity of 480 MVA, but it was later increased and now has a capacity of 720 MVA. The interconnection enhances the security of supply to both companies and produces cost savings by the economical interchange of electricity and the reduction of operating reserve requirements (CLP 1991). In recent years, CLP has expanded its business to property development. A chart showing the structure of the electricity industry in Hong Kong is provided in Figure 2.2.

(5) *Concluding Remarks*

In conclusion, we can divide the historical development of the Hong Kong electricity industry into three distinct periods. The first period is before 1964 when both companies were not under any government control on price or profit. The second period is from 1964 to 1978, during which CLP was under the Scheme of Control. The third period is from 1979 onwards, when both companies were under the Scheme of Control. This division coincides with Hong Kong's economic development.

Before the early 1950s, Hong Kong relied heavily on the entrepôt trade to earn income. The United Nations' embargo on communist China, placed when the Korean War broke out, forced Hong Kong to develop its own industries. The demand for electricity, particularly industrial demand, increased significantly. Industrialists played an important role in Hong Kong's industrialization process and they were in the frontline to lobby for government control of the two electricity companies.

During the second period, Hong Kong's industries, together with the demand for electricity, continued to grow at a rapid pace. The growth momentum was hampered somewhat by the 1973 oil crisis, which caused a great increase in the price of fuel and electricity. The Government subsequently introduced quantity controls on the use of electricity. Despite this, Hong Kong's economy recovered rapidly in 1976.

In 1978, the Scheme of Control for CLP was renewed and China announced its open door policy. As a result, more and more factories relocated from Hong Kong to China. Hong Kong transformed itself gradually from an industrial city to a services centre. This transformation process was clearly shown by the decline in industrial demand and increase in commercial demand for electricity.

Figure 2.2 The Hong Kong Electricity System, 1995

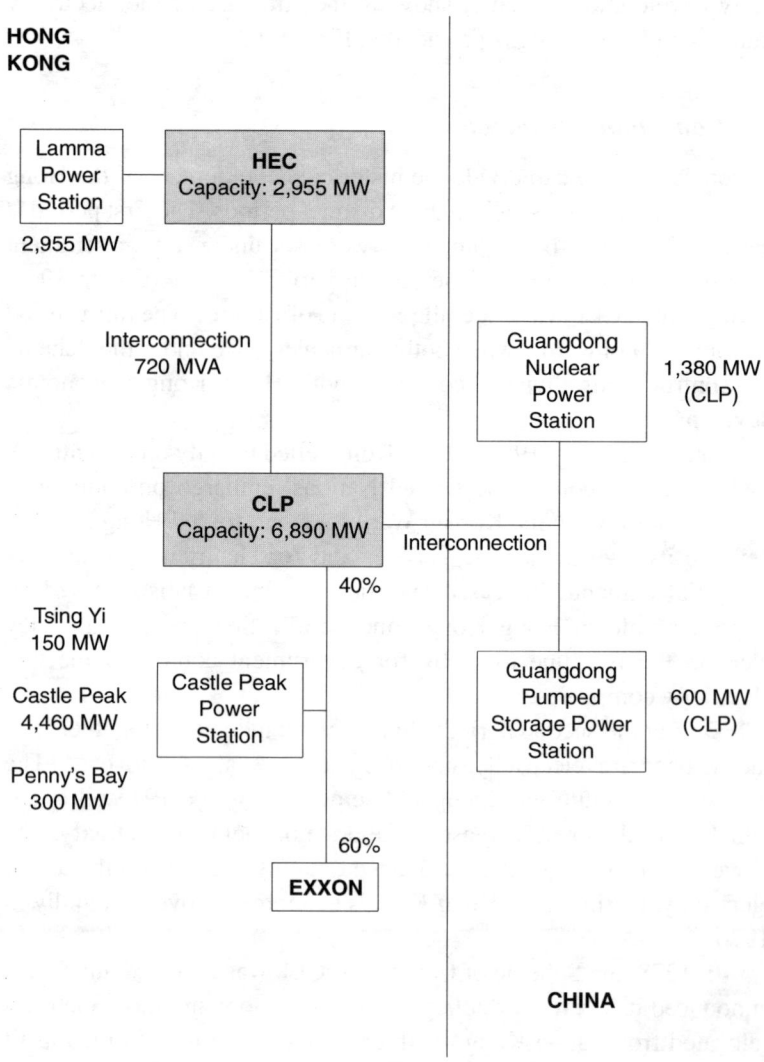

2.2 Government Monitoring Arrangements

The expansion of the two companies in the 1980s was not without obstacles. In January 1980, CLP raised its basic tariff for the first time since 1974 by an average of 2.6 cents per kWh. The company explained that the increase was due to the substantial capital expenditure required to meet the increased demand during the 1980s, and financing arrangements, including extensive loans, which had been made to meet this expansion. The loans were supported by the Export Credits Guarantee Department of the United Kingdom. The loans were set at fixed interest rates ranging between 7.25% to 8.5%, and would be repayable within 8.5 to 12 years from the dates of commissioning the capital assets (CLP 1979–1981). Concurrent with the tariff revision, CLP appointed Ebasco Business Consulting Company, a New York-based company with extensive international experience, to undertake an overall review of load management and to determine how consumers could be encouraged to transfer their demand for electricity from peak to off-peak periods.

Taking into account the recommendations made by Ebasco, CLP revised its tariff again in January 1981. The average charge per kWh increased sharply from 34.1 cents to 49.9 cents. Of the increase, 11.5 cents was due to higher oil prices (CLP 1981). In January 1982, CLP increased its basic tariff by an average of 5.5 cents per kWh and a further increase of 5 cents was implemented in January 1983 (CLP 1982). HEC also revised its basic tariff upwards drastically in these few years.

The tariff increases caused great public resentment and again there was a call for public monitoring. Demonstrations and protests against these rate increases were led by students and the Federation of Hong Kong Industries. The industrialists, who had benefited from CLP's policy of subsidizing industry, protested strongly against CLP's new rate policy which seemed to remove their privileges. Kadoorie, of CLP, suggested that there could be no question of changing the basic terms of the Scheme of Control before 1993, as the company had already arranged long-term loans on the security of the Scheme in its existing form (CLP 1982). On 24 November 1982, the

Legislative Council, after a lengthy debate, decided to rule out any public monitoring, arguing that this would duplicate the monitoring which was being implemented by the Government. Nine years later, in 1991, when the Hong Kong Government held discussions with public utilities about their future, a conflict of interests between the utilities and their customers arose again. On 13 November 1991, the Legislative Council ruled out any consultation with the public, but would "consider" their opinions before reaching new agreements with the utilities (*Ming Pao*, 14 November 1991).

In 1982, HEC recommended that the Government disclose the full details of the Scheme of Control under which it operated, in the belief that this would give the public a clearer understanding of the monitoring system imposed by the Government. Full details of the Scheme, together with those of certain other utilities, were published in late 1982 and were available to the public (HEC 1982). CLP welcomed the publication (CLP 1982).

Amid the protests against higher tariffs, the Government appointed consultants, Burns & Roe Inc. in 1982, to review the technical aspects of system planning by the two companies. After almost a year of study, the consultants submitted their report in mid-1983. An executive summary of the Report was subsequently made available to the public (CLP 1983). The Report confirmed that the two companies' planning had been soundly based, properly applied, and that their generation development plans would provide a reliable and adequate supply without over-expansion. In 1983, the Government appointed independent consultants, Ernst & Whinney, to assess the Government's arrangement for monitoring the two electricity companies and to recommend various means to further enhance the government's monitoring capabilities. A consultancy report was published in March 1985. The consultants concluded that the Government's monitoring system in the past had been adequate and appropriate to ensure compliance with the terms of the Schemes of Control (Hong Kong Government 1986 & 1989). Nevertheless, they also recommended a number of steps to strengthen the monitoring process. The recommendations were later considered by a special working party responsible to the Secretary for Economic Services. One recommendation that the Government immediately adopted was that the consultants would be retained to examine the technical aspects of future financing plans submitted by the two electricity companies. The working party submitted its report to the Executive Council in 1987, and the consultants' recommendations have since been implemented (Hong Kong Government 1989).

As shown in the consultancy report (Ernst and Whinney 1984), there is no particular commission or committee responsible for the monitoring work. Several government organizations share the monitoring responsibilities, they are:

(1) Treasury Financial Monitoring Unit

The unit is headed by a Chief Treasury Accountant and is responsible for the review of policy regarding financial monitoring of public utilities and providing financial advice regarding public utilities to the Secretary for Economic Services.

(2) Economic Services Branch

The branch is headed by the Secretary for Economic Services and is responsible for developing and recommending government economic policies, including energy and electricity matters. The Secretary for Economic Services is accountable to the Financial Secretary. The Branch has two divisions: Services and Analysis. The Energy Subdivision of the Economic Services Division receives professional assistance on the economic and financial side from the Economic Analysis Division and Financial Monitoring Unit, and then makes recommendations to the Secretary for Economic Services, and ultimately to the Executive Council.

(3) Electrical and Mechanical Services Department

The department is responsible for providing technical input on financial plans and conducting major reviews of power company expansion plans. The Department responds to the Economic Services Branch for policy guidance.

While confirming that the existing monitoring structure was adequate and appropriate, the consultants recommended that there should be written procedures for precise specifications of monitoring responsibilities. They recommended that the Economic Services Division should continue to coordinate the overall monitoring effort. This division of labour in monitoring continues today.

2.3 Salient Features of the Scheme of Control

In this section, we outline the main features of the Scheme of Control which governs the operations of the two electricity companies in Hong Kong. We also attempt to highlight the problems arising from the terms stipulated in *The Schemes of Control* (Hong Kong Government 1982b).[6]

(1) A Long-Term Contract

The Scheme of Control can be regarded as a long-term contract between the Government and the two electricity companies. The duration of the contract is 15 years. The contract exists, as stated at the beginning of *The Schemes of Control*, because "certain companies provide services to the public in a monopoly or semi-monopoly situation. This makes it necessary, in the 'public interest', for the Government to establish certain guidelines (known as Schemes of Control) under which the companies will operate." (p. 2)

To induce private investment in the electricity industry, "the Government recognizes that the Companies and their shareholders are entitled to earn a return which is reasonable in relation to the risks involved and the capital invested in and retained in the business, and in return, the Government has to be assured that service to the consuming public continues to be adequate to meet demand, to be

---

6. The references of the terms are in parentheses.

efficient and of high quality, and is provided at the lowest cost which is reasonable in the light of financial and other considerations." (pp. 5 and 75)

The capital assets used in the supply of electricity are immobile, specialized to the electricity industry, and extremely long-lived. Also, construction of electricity supply facilities takes years to complete. Once a commitment to invest is made, a great portion of the investment becomes a sunk cost with very low value in alternative uses. In other words, there is a problem of policy credibility; electricity companies face uncertainty over the value of their assets, as the Government can affect their value by changing its policy. The result is under-investment in the industry. Long-term contracts with the Government provide a relatively more stable environment for electricity companies to make long-term investments in electricity supply.

However, the idiosyncratic nature of the assets used in the industry may also encourage opportunistic behaviour by the electricity companies when the contracts are renegotiated. During the three years prior to the expiry of the contracts, the Government institutes discussions with the companies regarding the revision and extension of the Schemes of Control (pp. 9 and 79). The situation then becomes one of bilateral negotiations. As the setting up of alternative systems of electricity supply takes time, the existing companies are able to behave opportunistically. They can ask for better terms (e.g. higher permitted rate of return) which may not be acceptable to the Government. The Government is in a lock-in position with few alternatives. For example, when the Government made a new long-term contract with CLP in 1978 the company successfully raised the permitted rate of return on equity from 13.5% to 15%.

The Scheme of Control does not grant monopoly rights to the existing companies, and new companies can legally enter into the industry.[7] However, high set up costs and scale economies enjoyed

---

7. Bus and telephone companies in Hong Kong have entered into separate franchise and Scheme of Control agreements with the Government.

by incumbent firms may effectively prevent new companies from entering. The electricity industry is a frequently cited example of a natural monopoly. A single firm can provide all of the output at a lower total cost than could be achieved by having more than one firm. Also, as a high sunk cost is incurred in production, the electricity market is not contestable. Therefore, potential competition or threat of entry may not effectively induce the existing firms to behave competitively.

At present, HEC supplies to a smaller geographical area in Hong Kong and has a smaller scale of production. If scale economies is a reason for a natural monopoly to exist, then we should favour the merging of HEC and CLP on the grounds that it will yield larger economies of scale. The average tariff of HEC has been higher than that of CLP, and the tariff differential has been growing in recent years. It has been argued that the merging of the two companies could lower overall tariffs and allow people living on Hong Kong Island to enjoy the same tariffs as people in areas served by CLP. But before advocating this, we must discern carefully which stages of electricity production would bring substantial scale economies and provide a case for natural monopoly.

(2) Rate-of-Return Regulation

Under the existing Schemes of Control, HEC and CLP are permitted to earn a rate of return of 13.5% of the average net fixed assets, plus 1.5% of shareholders' investment made within the effective period of the contracts (pp. 7 and 76). In other words, the permitted rates of return for debt capital and equity capital are 13.5% and 15%, respectively.

Apart from the problem of rate base valuation, a basic problem arising from this rate-of-return regulation is how these permitted rates of return are determined. The permitted return should be set at a level which allows "these companies and their shareholders to earn a return which is reasonable in relation to the risks involved and the capital invested in and retained" in the electricity supply business. A correct choice of permitted rate of return is pertinent to inducing efficient production and providing incentives for the companies to make future investments.

A development fund was created under the Scheme of Control. If the two electricity companies earn less than the permitted return, the deficiency will be compensated from the development fund. Conversely, if they earn more than the permitted return, the excess will be transferred to the development fund (pp. 7 and 77). Therefore, although the main purpose of the fund is to assist in financing the acquisition of fixed assets, it seems to serve as a buffer to guarantee permitted return to the two companies.

If the companies expect that the development fund (after deducting the amount to meet the companies' full financial commitments) is insufficient to cover the deficiency, they can apply for tariff increases (pp. 19–21 and 89–90). Government approval of tariff increases should be sought if the increase is in excess of 0.8 cents per kWh, otherwise, the increase is automatic. Apart from gaining Government approval, a financial review should be conducted if the increase is in excess of 1.6 cents per kWh.

On the contrary, an amount equal to 8% of the average of the opening and closing balances of the development fund will be transferred from the permitted return to the rate reduction reserve (pp. 8 and 77). The balance of the reserve, if exceeding the total of the amount transferred for the current year and the three preceding years, will be used to reduce, by means of rebates, the tariffs charged to consumers in the following year.

Hence, for a price increase which does not exceed a certain limit, the adjustment is automatic. Moreover, when the development fund and rate reduction reserve exceed certain limits, the regulated firm has to reduce prices. This contrasts with the U.S. rate-of-return regulation, under which a regulatory lag exists in the price adjustment process. There is a general belief that under the traditional rate-of-return regulation, electricity prices have not risen (or fallen) fast enough to reflect changes in operating costs, construction costs and interest rates. One of the ways to tackle the problem of regulatory lag is through the use of a fuel adjustment clause in pricing. In Hong Kong, both electricity companies' tariff structures contain fuel adjustment clauses.[8]

A large part of operating costs in the supply of electricity lies in fuel costs. The inclusion of a fuel adjustment clause in the tariff structure can effectively transfer the risk of cost fluctuation from the electricity companies to the consumers. However, automatic fuel adjustment clauses have been criticized for providing poor incentive for electricity companies to minimize costs. Since any fuel cost increase can be passed on automatically to consumers through price increases, electricity companies are less likely to search for cheaper suppliers of fuel. They are also less inclined to build generators which are fuel efficient or which will economize on the use of fuel. To a large extent, the success of the Scheme of Control rests on its ability to encourage a regulated firm to lower its price without discouraging its incentive to make further investments at the same time.

(3) Organizational Structure

The two electricity companies are integrated firms. In the 1970s and 1980s, CLP owned (jointly with Exxon) Peninsula Electric Power Company Limited (PEPCO), Kowloon Electricity Supply Company Limited (KESCO), and Castle Peak Power Company Limited (CAPCO). Exxon supplied oil to these associated companies, and these companies in turn generated electricity which was sold exclusively to CLP. There was vertical integration in the fuel supply, generation, transmission, distribution and sale of electricity within CLP. In 1992, CAPCO acquired the shares and undertakings of PEPCO and KESCO and became a single associated generating

---

8. According to the tariff structures published by the two companies in the late 1980s and early 1990s, a corresponding fuel clause adjustment was to be made should the composite fuel price rise above or fall below $700 per gigajoules. But the tariff structures did not show the effect of higher thermal efficiency on fuel costs and prices of electricity.

company of CLP. In recent years, CLP has also diversified to other businesses, including property development, pumped storage development and electricity advisory services.

HEC is just one of the subsidiary companies of Hong Kong Electric Holdings Limited. The holding company not only engages in the supply of electricity, but also in property development, oil supply and the sale of electric appliances. Although the holding company was reorganized in 1987 to shed its non-electricity activities, such as property development, the company later participated in redeveloping its plant site at Ap Lei Chau into a private housing estate (South Horizons). Owing to the diversified nature of the holding company, the Government has added a special clause in the Scheme of Control with HEC relating to Group Transactions (p. 78).

The Scheme of Control and the permitted rates of return apply only to electricity-related activities. "Electricity-related" refers to any act, matter or thing directly or indirectly appertaining to the generation, transmission, distribution and sale of electricity (pp. 10 and 80). However, in practice, it is not often easy to distinguish whether a transaction is electricity-related or not. Vertically-integrated firms may practise transfer pricing in order to increase the total profit obtained from their subsidiaries or associated companies. The consumers of electricity may end up paying higher tariffs than the justifiable levels under the Scheme of Control.

The mechanics of the Scheme of Control become even more complicated when a company like CLP engages in both selling electricity to China and purchasing electricity from joint-venture companies established in China. In the former situation, it seems that CLP has overexpanded as it has excess electricity to sell. In the latter situation, it is possible for CLP to shift profits from Hong Kong to an unregulated company located in China, and then request that its tariff be raised in Hong Kong when it earns less than the permitted return (Liu 1990). The regulator has to prevent an integrated firm from adopting pricing policies which would raise its level of profits.

(4) Financial Structure

Under the Scheme of Control, the financing arrangements for future expansion of the electricity companies should be submitted for review and agreement by the Government (pp. 8 and 78). Apart from debt and equity financing, the companies can acquire assets through the development fund. A charge of 8% per annum on the average balance of the development fund and interest payable, up to a maximum of 8% per annum on long-term financing, will be deducted from the permitted return (pp. 7 and 76).

The choice of 8% is quite interesting and an immediate question is how this rate is determined. Nevertheless, the existence of the development fund, together with the arrangements in the deduction of permitted return, must have an impact on the financial structure of the two electricity companies. The financing arrangements as well as the debt-equity ratios of the companies must have been affected by such arrangements.

2.4 Renegotiations in the Early 1990s

As the old Scheme of Control was due to expire at the end of 1993, the Government started negotiations with the two electricity companies concerning the terms of their new Schemes of Control in 1991 and 1992. The public at large initiated several alternatives for the Government to consider in order to protect the customers and to promote efficiency in the electricity industry. These alternatives are briefly summarized below.

(1) Merging of the Two Companies

It appears that the merging of the two companies would lead to greater efficiency in the generation of electricity and cost-savings from larger economies of scale.[9] The networks of the two companies have been

---

9. One of the advocates of the merging of the two companies is Dr. Liu Pak-wai, of the Chinese University of Hong Kong. See *The Other Hong Kong Report 1990* (Hong Kong: The Chinese University Press, 1990), pp. 339–345.

interconnected since 1981 for the purpose of mutual backup in the event of emergency. Merging would also allow economic interchange of electricity which would result in cost-savings. It is expected that full integration of the networks of the two companies would generate even larger cost-savings. But the basic problem is how the Government induces two private companies to join together. The two companies already failed to reach an agreement on merging in the early 1960s, yet if integration would reduce costs and raise profits, then there is no economic reason why the two companies would not voluntarily do so.

(2) Restructuring

Some interest groups have long argued for the scrapping of the Scheme of Control. They argue that the Scheme has been protecting the electricity companies rather than the consumers. They felt that the two companies should not be guaranteed permitted rates of return. However, if the Scheme of Control was abandoned, what would be the alternative? One alternative would be the restructuring of the whole industry which would allow free competition in certain stages (e.g. generation) in the production of electricity. The geographical boundaries in the supply of electricity could be removed. The interconnection of power systems makes it possible for CLP and HEC to compete and to supply electricity to all areas of Hong Kong.

(3) Maintaining the Status Quo

Both the Government and the two companies argue that the existing system functions very well. Electricity prices in Hong Kong are low compared to those in other countries. Reliability of supply is high with very few major outages. The terms under the Scheme of Control, including the permitted rates of return, ensures sufficient investment in the industry to be beneficial for the future growth of the economy.

Unlike the telephone company in Hong Kong, the two electricity companies are not in favour of using indexing or price-cap (e.g.

RPI-X formula) to price electricity. They argue that the price increases of electricity in the 1980s were well below the increases in the consumer price index (*Ming Pao*, 14 November 1991). The Scheme of Control has also helped the companies to issue low-interest debt. Restricting the electricity companies to raise prices according to a formula would cause financial difficulties to the existing companies in times of rapid capital expansion.

2.5 Concluding Remarks

After lengthy negotiations, the Government eventually decided to renew the Scheme of Control for the two electricity companies (for another 15 years, i.e. lasting until 2008). In broad terms, the new Scheme remains more or less the same as its predecessor. However, it was agreed between the two companies and the Government that the period over which fixed assets would be depreciated was to be increased in order to reflect more accurately the expected useful life of assets. Both companies are now obliged to promote demand-side management and energy conservation. Furthermore, the Government has made a concession to CLP, by allowing it to keep 20% of the profits derived from selling electricity to China.

Once CLP and Exxon had signed the contract with the Government, they announced the decision to spend up to HK$60 billion over the next decade on a new plant at Black Point with a capacity of 6,000 MW, which is the largest one in the world under active planning. The first unit is to be commissioned in 1996. Similar to the previous Scheme, CLP would rely on long-term loans (fixed interest rates ranging between 5% and 10.5%) to finance the project. In addition, the company signed a contract with the Chinese Government for the supply of natural gas from Hainan. This huge capital expansion (about half of the expenditure on the new airport in Hong Kong) and the reliance on debt financing would imply a much higher permitted return (and tariffs) in the coming few years. The other electricity company, HEC, has also submitted its plan to construct a new power plant on Po Toi Island.

Similar to the previous Schemes, the new agreements contain a five year review clause. This enables either party, the Government or the regulated electric utility, to ask for a revision of the terms in the agreement. Such a request should be made before the end of the company's financial year in 1998. Hence, despite the fact that both companies are now operating under the new Scheme of Control, the Hong Kong Government can still initiate changes in the terms of the Schemes. Over the past years, the operating environment of the energy industry has changed rapidly. It is hoped that our study will provide information for the regulator in Hong Kong on how to improve the existing control scheme.

CHAPTER 3

Regulatory Systems in the United States and the United Kingdom

Before evaluating the effects of the Scheme of Control in Hong Kong, it is important to distinguish between the control system in Hong Kong and the systems in the United States and the United Kingdom. Failing to do this could easily lead to incorrect conclusions being drawn from entirely different systems in other countries.

3.1 Rate-of-Return Regulation

(1) Regulatory Procedures in the United States

In the United States, state public utility commissions regulate the price and non-price terms and conditions of retail sales of electricity, while the Federal Energy Regulatory Commission (previously the Federal Power Commission) regulates wholesale sales made by investor-owned utilities. In most cases, investor-owned utilities operate as franchised monopolists serving retail customers in legally defined areas. The franchising process and terms of franchises vary from state to state. In a few areas, investor-owned utilities have overlapping franchises and, at least in theory, can compete with one another for customers (Joskow and Schmalensee 1983, p. 13). Most of these investor-owned utilities are subject to the rate-of-return regulation.

The rate-of-return regulation's ostensible aims are to protect the consumer and at the same time provide the company with a "fair" rate of return (Crew and Kleindorfer 1987). The regulatory process begins with a formal request made by a public utility for a change in the level or structure of its existing rates, accompanied by submission of evidence in support of the request. The utility must file its case and be prepared to be examined on it. Following the filing, the regulatory commission presides over a formal proceeding in which the evidence provided by the utility, along with evidence submitted by other parties such as commission staff and customers, is presented and examined. Intervenors, principally the state-appointed Rate Counsel, have the opportunity to object to the case, and then file their own testimony criticizing the case. The two sides, public utility and intervenors, may either discuss their differences and agree to a "stipulation" which has to be approved by the commission, or to litigate the case before an administrative law judge.

The litigation is similar to normal court proceedings in which cross-examination and rebuttal take place. After the hearings, the judge prepares a report which goes to the commission for a final decision. In some cases, the commission may use its own initiative to order an investor-owned utility to change the level and structure of the proposed tariffs, if the tariffs are found to be inconsistent with state law.

Most state commissions operate under a vague statutory mandate which states that the commission is to set prices that are "just, reasonable and non-discriminatory" (Joskow 1986, p. 4). State statute permits commissions to regulate the prices charged by investor-owned utilities, but not to fine or subsidize them. The basic principle of the rate-of-return regulation is that utilities should be allowed to charge prices which reflect "costs of service", if they are prudently incurred, and earn a fair rate of return on investment. The sum of all the approved costs of service is called the "revenue requirement", and prices are then set to generate revenue to meet this revenue requirement.

Different procedures are used by different regulatory commissions to estimate the costs and levels of service. Some base their estimates on costs from previous historical test years; others use forecasts of future costs (Kolbe *et al.* 1984, p. 5). Many commissions allow automatic price adjustments for some cost items, the most common being fuel cost. Prices are set at a level to allow the utility to earn a fair rate of return. In theory, the fair rate of return on investment should be high enough to compensate the owner of the utility properly for the cost of capital investment, properly adjusted for risk, and to provide incentives for utilities to raise capital in order to finance investments required to meet the demand for electric power efficiently (Joskow and Schmalenses 1983, p. 13).

The fair rate of return is an allowed, rather than a guaranteed rate of return. This is because the usual regulatory practice precludes "retroactive ratemaking" (going back and changing past prices to reflect actual costs). Economic conditions may change during the period the prices are in effect and, consequently, the regulated utility may earn less than the allowed rate of return. Therefore, the rate of return earned by the utility depends partly on the accuracy of the forecasts used to set prices, and partly on unforeseen developments. If the prices do not yield the allowed rate of return, then the utility may file another case for a price increase.

Several financial models have been used by regulatory commissions to estimate the cost of capital for regulated utilities. These models include the comparative earnings method, the dividend growth model, and the capital asset pricing model. Before the early 1980s, the comparative earnings method and the dividend growth model were preferred by many commissions. Recently, however, there is a tendency for more commissions to use the capital asset pricing model (CAPM).[1] In the past, when the dividend growth model was used, extrapolating historical accounting data was a common method of estimating dividend growth, but today this method has been replaced by estimates based on analysts' forecasts.

(2) Incentive Aspects of Rate-of-Return Regulation

In 1962, Averch and Johnson published their landmark paper dealing with monopolies subject to the rate-of-return regulation. According to the Averch-Johnson Proposition, if the allowed rate of return on

---

1. See Kolbe *et al.* 1984, pp. 122–123, and Water Services Association (UK) and Water Companies Association 1991, p. 28. A detailed discussion about the cost of capital concept will be provided in Chapter 6.

capital is between the profit-maximizing rate and the cost of capital, then the regulated firm will substitute capital for other factors of production and operate at an output at which cost is not minimized. The result is a non-optimal combination of resources. Several extensions and clarifications of the Averch-Johnson Proposition have been published, e.g. Wellisz 1963, Takayama 1969, Kafoglis 1969, Baumol and Klevorick 1970, Zajac 1970, Bailey and Malone 1970.

While discussion about the Averch-Johnson Proposition revolved around theoretical issues in the 1960s, attention was turned to empirical tests in the 1970s. Many statistical studies concerning the impact of the rate-of-return regulation have been published since 1973. They include studies by Spanne (1974), Courville (1974), Petersen (1975), Hayashi and Trapani (1976), and Boyes (1976). Nearly all of these studies provide some evidence to support the Averch-Johnson Proposition that the rate-of-return regulation produces inefficiencies in the choice of factor inputs.

These studies, however, were criticized by Murphy and Soyster (1983) for using a standard production function (with an index of fuel prices) without a separate representation of the fuel choice decision. The argument is that if more coal, instead of oil, is used, the fuel price index decreases while the proportion of expenditures on capital increases. The increase in capital expenditure is a result of using less expensive fuels which require more capital expenditure, rather than an indication of the presence of the Averch-Johnson effect. In Hong Kong, in the 1980s, the two electricity companies constructed coal-fired generators to replace their oil-fired ones. Although capital expenditure increased significantly, fuel cost decreased once these coal-fired generators had been completed. It is important to discern whether the rapid capital expansion is due to the Averch-Johnson effect or is simply the result of factor substitution for cost-minimization.

There are other empirical problems associated with the Averch-Johnson effect. Boyes (1976) argued that if the Averch-Johnson effect is true, then it should not be so difficult to get electric utilities to install pollution abatement equipment which would enlarge the rate base. Moreover, if fuel costs are automatically passed on to consumers, then electric power companies can choose investments combining lower capital costs with higher fuel costs. Thus, the automatic fuel adjustment clause should produce a negative Averch-Johnson effect.

Joskow (1986) criticized these theoretical and empirical studies on the Averch-Johnson effect as they failed to consider the actual regulatory process. In practice, regulatory commissions are not required to set prices which cover all costs incurred by regulated firms. Regulators have the authority to "disallow" capital costs (or any other costs) when setting rates, if they find the associated expenditures imprudent or unnecessary. This "threat of disallowance" would limit expenditures on "gold plating" (unnecessary capital expenditures), and would provide some incentive for the utility to make efficient investment decisions.

Furthermore, in practice, regulation does not take place in a continuous fashion. Prices are set for an interval of time, during which the utility is free to choose whatever input combination it likes. Bailey and Coleman (1971) found that the existence of regulatory lag induced utilities to reduce capital bias. Baumol and Klevorick (1970) also found that regulatory lag allowed utilities to keep the benefits of improved cost efficiency until they were asked by commissions to reduce prices in the next review. Joskow (1974) found that there was an asymmetry in the formal regulatory review. Utilities tended to ask for price increases when costs rose, but when costs fell they were often allowed to keep the existing prices and thus enjoyed higher rates of return. Hence, as a result of regulatory lag, the actual rates of return earned by utilities may be above or below the commission-determined fair rate of return.

(3) Rate-of-Return Regulation in the United States and Hong Kong

Do the above incentive features of the rate-of-return regulation exist in Hong Kong? Although electric utilities in the United States and Hong Kong are under the rate-of-return regulation, there are some differences in the regulatory procedures. First, utilities in Hong Kong are under formal long-term contracts which fix the nominal permitted rates of return for 15 years. In the United States, the nominal allowed rate of return is not fixed. When utilities think that the existing prices do not allow them to earn a fair rate of return on investment, they have to file formal requests for price increases. The nominal allowed rate of return depends on the results from financial models (such as CAPM) and other evidence (such as inflation rate) provided by a company to support its request. Second, there are no independent regulatory commissions or public hearings in Hong Kong; the regulatory duties are shared by various government departments. Third, so long as a balance exists in the development fund, the electric utilities in Hong Kong are guaranteed the permitted returns each year. In Hong Kong, regulatory lags do not exist; any return in excess of the permitted return is transferred to the development fund.[2]

An important distinction between the two rate-of-return systems is how the allowed rate of return is determined. In the United States, the allowed rate is based on a weighted average cost of capital, which takes into account the cost of equity and cost of debt; and the weights depend on the debt-equity ratio. In Hong Kong, the Government did not explain how the permitted rates of return were set (at 13.5% on debt capital and 15% on equity capital) or why the duration of the contract was fixed at 15 years. However, as we will see later, once the permitted rate of return based on fixed assets is set, the electric utilities can earn returns on equity in excess of the permitted level by adjusting the modes of financing.

At first sight, the Scheme of Control in Hong Kong, albeit incurring lower regulatory costs, tends to provide inadequate incentives

---

2. However, once the development funds have been depleted, permitted returns will no longer be guaranteed. Although the two electricity companies were able to earn the permitted returns every year, other companies under the Scheme of Control were not so fortunate. The two bus companies and the telephone company have earned less than the permitted returns in recent years, despite having been granted fare increases. In these few occasions, the development funds were insufficient to cover the shortfalls. In view of this, the permitted returns are not guaranteed. Price increases may not provide sufficient revenue for a regulated company to earn the permitted return. The effect of a price increase on returns depends on the price elasticity of demand.

for regulated firms to produce efficiently. Since the nominal rate of return is fixed, when the inflation rate fluctuates widely the Scheme may fail to fulfil the basic function of the rate-of-return regulation, which is to allow regulated firms to earn a return covering the cost of capital. The way in which the permitted return is set may also produce inefficient financing decisions.

On the other hand, it can be argued that such a long-term contract lowers risk, facilitates production plans and reduces transaction costs in production. Because of the nature of the electricity industry, government regulation is necessarily a long-term contract protecting both the producers and the consumers. In addition, the Scheme helps regulated companies to obtain debt financing at lower interest costs which, in turn, lowers the prices charged by the companies.

However, it can further be argued that the Scheme does not lower risk, but simply passes the risk on to consumers. Indeed, the fuel clause and price adjustment mechanism built into the Scheme allow the electricity companies to shift the burden of cost increases on to consumers. Even though the Scheme helps to obtain low-cost debt financing, the regulated companies may not be sharing the benefits with their consumers. These are not the only problems associated with this kind of rate-of-return regulation.

3.2 Problems with Rate-of-Return Regulation

As the major concern of the rate-of-return regulation is on equity and fairness, it is not surprising that outcomes are inefficient. Crew and Kleindorfer (1987) identify four categories for evaluating economic efficiency: allocative efficiency, X-efficiency, dynamic efficiency, and governance (or monitoring) cost efficiency.

(1) Allocative Efficiency

Allocative efficiency is the traditional measure of static efficiency. In a competitive market, prices are set so that total benefits less total costs (i.e. net benefits) are maximized. In general, maximization of net benefits requires that price equals marginal cost. However, because of scale economies, the need to cover costs and the non-existence of government subsidies, regulated prices are not likely to reflect marginal costs. Under the rate-of-return regulation, prices are based on average cost pricing or second-best pricing (such as Ramsey pricing), rather than true marginal cost pricing. Unless the regulator allows an efficient two-part tariff, the rate-of-return regulation can at best achieve only optimal second-best pricing.

(2) Productive Efficiency

Productive inefficiency or X-inefficiency is a concept introduced by Leibenstein (1966). It refers to the losses or wastes that occur when firms fail to combine inputs efficiently, which results in higher production costs. The possible Averch-Johnson effect suggests that regulated firms under the rate-of-return regulation use too much capital. In addition, such regulation is similar to a cost-plus contract which provides little incentive for regulated firms to minimize costs. This is because when they successfully reduce costs so that their returns exceed the allowed level, prices will be reduced in the next review. A firm under the rate-of-return regulation may intentionally spend more on staff and on "perks" for the management than necessary, as the firm can pass the cost on to consumers. Hence, it has been argued that the rate-of-return regulation fails to achieve productive efficiency. However, as mentioned above, the threat of disallowance and regulatory lag can mitigate such a disincentive effect.

(3) Dynamic Efficiency

Dynamic efficiency refers to the ability of the regulatory system to accommodate growth and change over time. A system is dynamically efficient if it is able to encourage the regulated firms to adopt innovation and invention, and to accommodate changes in tastes and preferences. The rate-of-return regulation is also deficient in dynamic efficiency. As profits are fixed, regulated firms have little incentive to adopt cost-saving innovations or to introduce new products.

In a competitive market, unregulated firms have to make investment decisions under conditions of uncertainty. Even though they have made efficient investment decisions *ex-ante*, they may end up earning more or less than a competitive return when demand and cost conditions change. Firms under the rate-of-return regulation, however, are not rewarded or penalized for unforeseeable fluctuations in demand or cost conditions. Even if a firm over-estimates demand and builds plants yielding excess capacity, it is still allowed to earn a rate of return on this excess capacity so long as it can defend its forecasting procedure. Thus the rate-of-return regulation punishes only bad decisions, not bad luck (Joskow 1986, p. 11). However, this does not eliminate risk, it simply transfers risk from the company to consumers. Consumers, whose interest is supposed to be represented by the regulator, have to bear all the risk from the investment decisions made by a regulated firm. Hence, the rate-of-return regulation also fails to allocate risk efficiently.

(4) Governance Cost Efficiency

In evaluating alternative governance structures for regulation, we have to consider the transaction costs involved. If a given governance structure requires considerable inputs (e.g. lawyers, accountants and regulators) to function properly, then these transaction costs must be included when measuring the net benefits. Governance costs are substantial under the rate-of-return regulation in the United States, as considerable resources are spent in the process of administrative hearings and litigations. MacAvoy's study (1970) suggests that the governance costs of regulatory proceedings instituted by the Federal Power Commission were larger than the net benefits warranted. With the huge amount of administrative expenditure at stake, the rate-of-return regulation also encourages wasteful rent-seeking activities (Crew *et al.* 1987). In the early 1960s, when the Hong Kong Government considered ways to control the two electric utilities, CLP made an appeal not to follow the U.S. system, for fears of substantial governance costs. In CLP's 1960 annual report, the Chairman wrote:

In order to secure simplicity in administration and to avoid undue interference with the detailed running of the Companies, it was decided to follow the British rather than the American tradition in electricity regulation; that is to say, the Agreement depends essentially on the application of a formula which remains in force for the duration of the Agreement, it is drafted so as to work with a minimum of formal administrative procedure.

When criticizing high governance costs of the system in the United States, we have to be aware of the trade-off between governance cost efficiency and transparency. As compared with the existing system in Hong Kong, the U.S. system is more transparent, customers have better access to information and can argue against price increases. In Hong Kong, there is less transparency and there are no public hearings on price increases. Regulated monopolists are only required to apply for price increases for final approval by the Executive Council. If the regulatory agencies think that a price increase is justified, they will recommend the Executive Council approve it. This process, though less adversarial in public, can also be costly if it arouses protests by consumer groups and grass roots organizations (Liu 1991).

(5) Other Problems

There are other problems associated with the U.S. regulatory system. For example, there is a problem with asymmetric information, as utility managers are always better informed than regulators. Regulators are not generally very keen in distinguishing efficient from inefficient behaviour. They simply do not have enough necessary information to detect all flawed decisions in a way that would satisfy legal standards for disallowances. Utility managers have every incentive to make their decisions seem prudent by arguing that poor performance is due to bad luck, rather than bad decisions. Also, if the threat of disallowance is not credible, a regulated utility will have diminished incentive to supply electricity efficiently.

Finally, if price increases lag behind cost increases, regulatory lags may worsen the financial situations of regulated firms rather than provide incentives for them to lower costs. In the 1970s, as factor prices increased rapidly and further savings due to productivity growth and scale economies disappeared, regulatory lag became a less important way to increase efficiency. Rate cases were more frequent and automatic adjustment clauses, especially for fuel, became very important (Joskow 1986). During the 1970s, the real earnings of many electric power companies in the United States declined and their stock prices fell, because the regulated prices were not adequate to compensate investors for the capital they provided in a world of rapid inflation. Electric power companies were reluctant to invest in new generating plants. The U.S. Government then passed the Public Utility Regulatory Policies Act of 1978 (PURPA) which encouraged cogeneration.

Cogeneration is the process of generating electricity as a by-product in the manufacturing of other goods, such as paper or steel. By-product electricity can be used by its producers and/or sold to another party (Fox-Penner 1990). The PURPA, among other things, required utilities to buy power at regulatory-determined prices from cogenerators, small power producers and renewable fuel users whose generating facilities were found by the FERC to be "qualified facilities". The Act guarantees qualified facilities the right to sell self-made power back to the nearest utility at the latter's full avoided cost. FERC defined avoided cost as the incremental cost to an electric utility of electric energy or capacity, or both, which, but for the purchase from the cogenerator, such utility would generate itself or purchase from another source (Berry 1989). Although cogeneration technology predated PURPA by many decades, the act broke the monopoly bottle-neck in the transmission and encouraged competition in the generation of electricity. To enhance competition, cogenerating facilities could not be more than 49% utility-owned. Because the avoided cost of monopoly utilities was so much higher than the cost of electricity from cogeneration, the PURPA policy led to a massive oversupply in generating capacity and stabilized prices of electricity in many states during the 1980s (Summerton and Bradshaw 1991). The PURPA also directly and indirectly encouraged self-generation and wheeling. Since all states except Texas have an interconnected grid, FERC retains regulatory jurisdiction over whole-sale wheeling.

To encourage further competition in the generation business, the Energy Policy Act of 1992 (EPAct) lifted some of the restrictions imposed by the Public Utility Holding Company Act (PUHCA) of 1935 on utility diversification and created a new category of corporation, "exempt wholesale generators" (EWGs). EWGs are defined roughly as companies that own generators and sell electricity exclusively at wholesale level anywhere in the world or at retail level outside the United States. As these new power producers are not considered "electric utilities", they are exempt from most PUHCA requirements. The EPAct also gave FERC broad authority to mandate wholesale transmission access. Combined with the actions of state commissions to restructure the electric industry, the Act enhances competition at the wholesale and retail levels. The Act made it possible for retail customers to exit from their franchised utility and buy electricity from other areas at more attractive prices.

The restructuring process in the U.S. electric power industry resulted in the problem of stranded costs (investment rendered useless because of open competition) incurred by franchised monopolists. There is still a debate about whether these monopoly utilities should be compensated for their loss of revenue. If compensation is required, there is also a question of the extent to which they are to be compensated. It is proposed that an efficient exit fee be charged on those customers who exit from their franchised utility. As the existing transmission systems are owned by different entities, the opening up of the transmission grid for equal access has also brought about the issues of ownership and control of transmission.

The many shortcomings of the rate-of-return regulation prompted interest in the incentive regulation in the 1980s. In recent years, theories of regulation have been mainly in the area of incentive contracts between regulated firms and the government. In the next section we will consider one of these incentive contracts, namely the price-cap regulation, which is now widely used in U.K. privatized industries.

3.3 Price-Cap Regulation

(1) The Origin of Price-Cap Regulation

In 1982, the U.K. Government announced its plan to privatize British Telecommunications (BT). The framework of the privatization programme was laid down in the White Paper, *The Future of Telecommunications in Britain.* Given BT's monopoly position in the industry, the prospect of privatization should have been accompanied by some form of regulation to contain its market power. The Department of Industry's original intention was to adopt a modified rate-of-return regulation (Beesley and Littlechild 1989), but Professor Alan Walters, the Prime Minister's Economic Adviser at the time, argued fiercely against it (Vickers and Yarrow 1988). He argued that it was similar to 100% taxation, provided poor incentives for innovation and efficiency, and that the American experience showed that the system was wasteful, bureaucratic and inefficient.

With other regulatory options under debate, a study was commissioned by Professor Stephen Littlechild of Birmingham University at the end of 1982. His report in early 1983 recommended a local tariff reduction (LTR) scheme, better known as the RPI-X proposal. After further discussions and investigations, this control on prices, or price cap, was finally adopted, and variants of it have been used for other privatized utilities, including electric utilities.

The key features of the price-cap regulation are:

(a) The regulator directly sets a ceiling for prices to be charged by the regulated firm according to a formula: the average price of a specified basket of services must not exceed RPI-X (rate of change in retail price index minus X), where X is an adjustment factor to share productivity gains between the company and the consumers. In other words, the prices of the regulated services must fall in real terms by X percent per annum.

(b) For a specified period of time (usually several years), the regulated firm may set prices freely below the ceilings.

(c) Price-ceilings are defined for baskets of services provided by the regulated firm. There may be different price ceilings for different baskets of services.

(d) The adjustment factor X is specified by the government and will be reviewed and possibly changed at the end of the specified period.

(e) The regulator can adjust the factor X in any review or interim-review. The regulator may modify this RPI-X constraint in the regulated company's licence at any time by agreement with the licensee. If the licensee does not agree, the regulator may refer the matter to the Monopolies and Mergers Commission (MMC).

(2) Arguments For and Against Price-Cap Regulation

In a paper written by Beesley and Littlechild (1989), they summarized the arguments for and against the price-cap regulation. First, they suggested that RPI-X is more efficient than the rate-of-return regulation. It is less vulnerable to "cost-plus" inefficiency and over-capitalization (the Averch-Johnson effect). This is because the regulated firm can keep whatever profits it earns during the specified period, but it must also accept any losses, thus there is an incentive to produce as efficiently as possible. As efficiency increases, it is possible for both the company and the consumers to benefit. The company enjoys higher profits while the consumers buy at lower prices. Since regulated companies keep all profits, they have a greater incentive to innovate and to introduce new products, resulting in higher dynamic efficiency than under the rate-of-return regulation.

Second, RPI-X allows the company greater flexibility to adjust the structure of prices, as there is no price control on services outside the basket. As a result, the regulated firm can adopt pricing arrangements to achieve optimal second-best pricing. Within the specified period under the existing price-cap, the firm can learn the cost structure and then adjust the price structure accordingly.

Third, it is argued that RPI-X is easier to operate and its governance costs are lower than the U.S. rate-of-return regulation. Both regulators and company can devote less resources to operate the system. It is also more transparent as the system focuses on prices, which are of greater concern to customers. Customers are guaranteed that price increases are under some form of controls. Hence, the system also helps to curb inflation and, being less discretionary, the price-cap also has less danger of regulatory capture.

Like all regulatory systems, the price-cap has its shortcomings. Many of the arguments put forward against the price-cap revolve around the setting of the X-factor. First, the X factor has to be set and reset repeatedly, in order to secure a reasonable rate of return to the regulated firm. In addition to the production cost and cost of capital, this process requires information on productivity gains. If the X factor is not set appropriately, inefficiencies will arise. In addition, there would be political pressure from the company and consumers in setting and resetting the X factor. Any shift in the X factor in favour of one group (customers) will be at the expense of the other (shareholders).

Vickers and Yarrow (1988) argued that the price-cap formula lacks any long-term guarantees as to the decisions that will be taken when they come to be reviewed. In the absence of clear guidance as to the long-term conduct of regulatory policy, private investors may be concerned that they will not be able to recover the cost of capital. Hence, because of the lack of credibility with respect to future government policy, there would be a real danger of under-investment in a privatized industry. The cost of capital (and prices) may be raised by the presence of this regulatory risk.

Second, companies may believe that any increase in efficiency in the short term will invite a tougher X factor in later periods, or even induce an adverse change of the X factor within the current period. If the short-term gain is more than offset by the long-term loss, they will avoid increasing productivity. This is similar to the problem of the ratchet effect in the contract made between a socialist firm and the state.

Third, some people question whether the price-cap actually has greater price flexibility and transparency. Under the rate-of-return regulation, the regulatory procedure, which involves public hearings and litigations, should be more transparent. Greater price flexibility may be a disadvantage rather than an advantage since it allows price discrimination and cross-subsidization. As costs of various services are difficult to determine precisely, price discrimination and cross-subsidization cannot be easily detected.

Lastly, as the price-cap focuses on prices, regulated firms may shirk on quality. Therefore, the regulator has to incur costs to closely monitor the quality of service (Liu 1991, p. 270).

(3) Price-Cap Regulation in the Electricity Supply Industry (ESI)

After the Conservative Party came to power in 1979, there was a shift in U.K.'s energy policy. The 1983 Energy Act attempted to introduce some competition into generation and supply by liberalizing third party access to the then nationalized transmission and distribution networks. The Area Boards, which were public corporations responsible for the distribution of electricity in their regions, were also required to buy electricity from sources other than the Government's Central Electricity Generating Board (CEGB). But the Act had little effect on the ESI: no private generator made any form of arrangement to sell electricity to a distant consumer through the networks. The Act failed to attract new entrants because of the anti-competitive behavior of the CEGB in adjusting the cost or price (Vickers and Yarrow 1988; 1991a). In February 1988, the British Government published two White Papers to restructure the ESI in England and Wales. The main features of the new structure were:

(a) The division of non-nuclear power stations owned by the CEGB between two new companies: National Power and PowerGen.

(b) The sale of the 12 Area Boards, which were renamed Regional Electricity Companies (RECs) and became licensees in March 1990. RECs have two separate businesses: distributing electricity from the Grid and supplying electricity to consumers. Entry to supply is free while entry to distribution is not.

(c) Transmission is separated from generation, and is carried out by the new National Grid Company (NGC), which is jointly owned by the 12 privatized RECs. The wires owned by NGC and the RECs must be made available for use by third parties at regulated prices. The NGC is responsible for dispatching power stations in accordance with arrangements for the power "pool" (under the Pooling and Settlements Agreement), which is the new wholesale market for power. RECs can enter into generation to a limit of 15% of their requirements. The entry to generation is free.[3]

The framework for regulation later appeared in the 1989 Electricity Act. The Act sets up the Office of Electricity Regulation (OFFER) to regulate the industry. Its head is the Director General of Electricity Supply (DGES). Professor Stephen Littlechild, who first advocated the price-cap regulation, is OFFER's first Director. His main duties are to ensure that demands for electricity are met and that licensees can finance their activities, to monitor licence conditions and to promote competition in generation and supply. Licence conditions could be changed either by agreement with the licensee, or by the DGES successfully making a reference to the Monopolies and Mergers Commission (MMC), the U.K. competition authority (Vickers and Yarrow 1991a). The price-caps imposed on the privatized firms are as follows:

(a) The price charged by the National Grid Company for the use of its system is capped according to an "RPI minus X" formula. The X factor in the cap is determined in a way to allow a regulated firm to share the benefit from increased efficiency. If the productivity of the regulated firm is increased at a rate faster than the X factor, then the firm can keep the excess returns. The excess returns will only be eliminated in the next regulatory review.

---

3. Following the privatization of RECs, National Power, PowerGen and NGC in England and Wales, the two vertically-integrated electricity companies in Scotland, Scottish Power and Scottish Hydroelectric, were also privatized in 1991.

(b) The price charged by each REC takes the form of RPI plus X, with the X terms varying among RECs (depending on their investment requirements).

(c) The price charged to consumers with peak demand less than 10 MW is subject to RPI − X + Y regulation. The Y factor reflects the cost to the REC of electricity purchases, transmission and distribution, and a fossil fuel levy. These cost components are beyond the control of the REC.

So the ESI in England and Wales was subject to substantial restructuring before privatization. The British Government has adopted a structure of vertical separation. This new structure aims to promote competition in the generation and supply of electricity and to prevent abuse of market power in transmission and distribution by means of the price-cap regulation. Competition in the supply business which was initially restricted to large users, was intended to gradually be expanded to small users. However, it is evident that the duopolists (National Power and PowerGen) in power generation have exercised their market power to raise pool prices above marginal costs (Armstrong *et al.* 1994). Competition in generation also brings concern about excessive investment in the building of gas-fired turbines. Conclusions drawn over the past few years have also suggested that competition in the supply market caused rebalancing in tariff structures in favour of larger industrial users (Yarrow 1994).

3.4 Price-Cap Regulation and Rate-of-Return Regulation

It may be helpful to consider how the price-cap regulation in the United Kingdom differs from the rate-of-return regulation in the United States (see Waterson 1990, and Weyman-Jones 1990). In the first place, under the price-cap regulation, the periods between reviews are known and fixed in advance. This means that the period of cost risk is not under the control of the regulated firms, instead it is predetermined by the regulator. Under the U.S. rate-of-return regulation, the regulated firm will ask for a rate review if they think they can justify it. So the risk period is endogenous, rather than exogenous, under the U.S. system.

In the regulatory process, there is no requirement that regulators in the United Kingdom look at past costs in setting prices. Regulators may take their own estimates of future costs into account. So the price-cap regulation is more forward-looking. In the U.S. rate-of-return regulation, historical costs are often used to justify rate changes (unless the test year is based on forecasts of future costs). The lack of restrictions on the information used by the regulators gives the price-cap regulation in the United Kingdom a greater degree of freedom than the U.S. rate-of-return regulation.

The governance costs of the two systems are also different. The U.K. regulators do not need to face judicial or court proceedings in determining prices. They can request a Monopolies and Mergers Commission audit of a utility's costs over a long period if disputes arise. The threat of requesting a MMC investigation serves as a bargaining tool to the regulators and increases the likelihood that regulated firms will report true costs. The U.S. regulators, however, do not possess this bargaining power. In addition, the regulatory commission framework in the United States is found to be more costly than the regulatory office approach in the United Kingdom. Considerable resources are devoted to public hearings in the United States. It is argued that the open hearings which allow information to be available to potential competitors, may also affect competition in the industry (Weyman-Jones 1990).

In the United Kingdom privatized ESI, price-cap regulations are in the forms of RPI – X, RPI + X and RPI – X + Y. RPI – X + Y regulation implies that a fraction of a utility's average price for a basket of outputs is assumed to depend on its own activities, and that these costs are capped by a growth rate equal to the rate of change in the retail price index minus a constant factor X. The remainder of the price is assumed to be determined by costs outside the utility's control (the Y factor) and these can be passed on to final consumers. Hence, the price-cap regulation preserves automatic adjustment clauses similar to those under the rate-of-return regulation. As a result, the incentive for regulated firms to minimize costs is reduced.

Furthermore, the setting of the price cap is not independent of the rate of return. In recent years, after the privatized electric utilities had announced great increases in profits, there was mounting political pressure to raise the X factor (i.e. to lower price). If regulators do not remain committed to the same X factor but change it during the current contractual period, this will affect the incentives of utilities to increase efficiency and will reduce the price-cap regulation to the rate-of-return regulation. Liston (1993) has reviewed the differences and similarities of the two systems and concluded that the price-cap in practice is not distinct from the rate-of-return regulation. In fact, it can be argued that the price-cap regulation is akin to the rate-of-return regulation with a longer regulatory lag (of several years). Braeutigam and Panzar (1993) also suggest that the choice between the price-cap and the rate-of-return regulation remains very much an empirical question.

Lastly, under the existing licence terms, privatized electric utilities are not allowed to engage in cross-subsidization. The generators' ability to engage in price discrimination is also limited by the requirement that they offer comparable terms to comparable purchasers. This provision extends to dealings between generation and supply businesses and also applies to RECs (Vickers and Yarrow 1991a). Hence, the price-cap regulation allows greater price flexibility without leading to cross-subsidization and discriminatory pricing. But Liston (1993) again argues that discrimination and cross-subsidization can still exist under the price-cap. As prices of different services are capped under a single ceiling, regulated firms may lower prices for some services and raise prices for other services, e.g. those with lower demand elasticities.

3.5 Concluding Remarks

The Scheme of Control in Hong Kong is a formal long-term contract between a private firm and the Government. The Scheme allows a regulated firm to enjoy certain permitted returns, in return for promised levels of services. The regulatory period is fixed at 15 years, which provides protection for regulated firms to earn sufficient returns to recover their sunk investment costs. Although the Scheme regulates the rates of return earned by public utilities, the regulatory process is entirely different from the rate-of-return regulation in the United States. Governance costs are lower under the Hong Kong system but there is also less transparency. In addition, the price adjustment mechanism is unlike the price-cap regulation in the United Kingdom. Prices charged by utilities under the Scheme are not capped. The two regulated electricity companies institute price decreases only when their development funds and rate reduction reserves exceed certain limits.[4] Bearing these differences in mind, we will evaluate the behaviours of regulated firms under the Scheme in the next chapter.

---

4. In 1994, apart from providing rebates to customers through the rate reduction reserve, CLP tried to reduce the tariff increase by means of a special rebate charged to the development fund.

CHAPTER 4

The Scheme of Control Mechanism

Debates on the Scheme of Control are centred around the development fund arrangement. It has been argued that the development fund provides regulated firms with a cheap source of finance, and breeds inefficiencies, as returns are guaranteed. The representatives from the regulated firms, on the other hand, counter-argue that the arrangement stabilizes the revenue and price of the service, and does not guarantee returns since there are interest costs and limits to drawing from the fund. As the development fund arrangement is an important feature of the Scheme of Control in Hong Kong, we begin this chapter with a detailed discussion of the operation of the fund.

4.1 Development Fund

(1) The Arrangement

The Scheme of Control requires each of the regulated companies to establish a development fund. The main purpose of the fund, as stated in the Scheme, is to assist in financing the acquisition of fixed assets. In addition, any difference between the (actual) profit after taxation and the permitted return will be transferred to or from the development fund (Figure 4.1). In other words, the regulated firm is not allowed to keep any excess profits above the permitted level. Any excess profits are to be put into the fund. The fund may be used for acquiring fixed assets, and interest accrued from the fund is to be transferred to a rate reduction reserve used for reducing tariffs. Thus, the development fund serves to finance expansion and stabilize the regulated firm's returns and prices.

It was agreed between the regulated firm and the Government

Figure 4.1   The Scheme of Control Mechanism

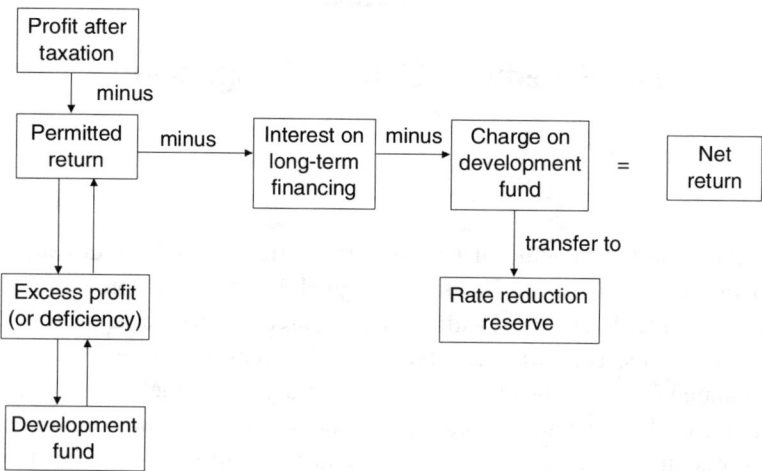

that the development fund would constitute a liability, not an asset, of the company. At present, the permitted rates of return on equity capital and debt (including the development fund) capital, are fixed at 15% and 13.5%, respectively. From the permitted return, the following interest deductions must be made in order to obtain the figure of net return:

— interest payable on long-term financing up to a maximum of 8% per annum; and
— a charge of 8% per annum on the average balance of the development fund to be credited to the rate reduction reserve, the purpose of which is to give rebates to consumers.

The net return is then distributed to shareholders of the company or retained for further investment. Tables 4.1 and 4.2 show the combined profit and loss statements of the two electricity companies under the Scheme of Control.[1] Both companies were able to earn the

---

1. Information about interest on fixed asset financing for HEC is not available for the period 1979–1981 because the company's accounting records have put the item together with tax adjustments.

Table 4.1 Combined Profit and Loss Statement of CLP, 1964–1994 (in HK$ million)

Year	Net revenue	Permitted return	Transfer to (from) D. F.	Deductions (1)	Deductions (2)	Net return	Development fund (D. F.)
1964	71	43	28	0	1	42	28
1965	86	53	33	0	4	50	61
1966	75	67	7	0	5	62	67
1967	90	83	7	0	6	77	75
1968	108	95	13	0	7	88	88
1969	123	107	16	0	8	99	104
1970	120	120	0	0	8	111	104
1971	123	134	(11)	0	8	126	92
1972	142	153	(11)	1	7	145	81
1973	169	172	(3)	1	6	165	78
1974	173	189	(16)	1	5	183	62
1975	187	208	(21)	2	5	201	63*
1976	253	222	31	2	6	214	94
1977	276	233	43	2	9	222	137
1978	312	253	59	2	13	238	197
1979	318	345	(27)	10	15	320	170
1980	581	586	(5)	92	13	481	164
1981	935	921	14	210	14	697	178
1982	1,349	1,299	50	364	16	919	228
1983	1,805	1,710	95	536	22	1,152	323
1984	2,292	2,166	126	677	31	1,458	449
1985	2,706	2,607	99	746	40	1,821	548
1986	3,418	3,011	407	779	60	2,172	955
1987	3,817	3,314	503	709	96	2,509	1,458
1988	3,904	3,504	400	618	132	2,754	1,858
1989	4,081	3,693	388	554	164	2,975	2,246
1990	4,448	3,984	464	470	198	3,316	2,710
1991	4,533	4,394	139	457	222	3,715	2,849
1992	5,118	4,745	373	455	243	4,047	3,222
1993	5,828	5,203	625	463	283	4,457	3,847
1994	5,385	5,878	(493)	511	272	5,095	2,944**

Notes: Deduction (1): Interest on long-term financing.
Deduction (2): Charge on development fund.
* Provisions for future profits tax HK$21m was credited because of the change in Inland Revenue Ordinance.
** A special rebate of HK$410m was given to customers in 1994 from the development fund.
Source: Annual reports of CLP, 1964–1994.

Table 4.2 Combined Profit and Loss Statement of HEC, 1979–1994 (in HK$ million)

Year	Net revenue	Permitted return	Transfer to (from) D. F.	Deductions (1)	Deductions (2)	Net return	Development fund (D. F.)
1979	208	208	0	N.A.	0	N.A.	0
1980	308	304	4	N.A.	0*	N.A.	4
1981	478	479	(1)	N.A.	0*	N.A.	3
1982	682	679	2	174	0*	505	5
1983	954	795	150	185	6	604	155
1984	968	865	103	178	17	670	258
1985	1,026	983	43	167	22	793	301
1986	1,200	1,166	34	220	26	920	335
1987	1,427	1,317	110	247	31	1,039	445
1988	1,441	1,461	(20)	104	35	1,322	425
1989	1,815	1,680	135**	187	39	1,454	560
1990	1,796	1,930	(134)	239	39	1,652	426
1991	2,275	2,228	47	303	36	1,889	473
1992	2,436	2,512	(76)	325	35	2,152	397
1993	2,821	2,848	(27)	359	31	2,458	370
1994	3,575	3,301	274	445	40	2,816	644

Notes: Deduction (1): Interest on fixed asset financing.
    Deduction (2): Charge on development fund.
    * Less than 0.5.
    ** In 1989, net revenue was HK$54m short of permitted return, the positive transfer arose from other non-recurrent adjustments, e.g. changes in the depreciation rates.

Source: Annual reports of HEC, 1979–1994.

permitted returns and the development funds of the two companies tended to increase over time.

(2) Auditing and Tariff Review[2]

Under the Scheme of Control, the financing arrangements for the

---

2. Our discussion is mainly based on the terms in the Schemes which govern the operations of the two electricity companies until 1993. For the details about the terms relating to auditing and tariff review, please refer to *The Schemes of Control* (Hong Kong Government 1982b), pp. 17–21 and pp. 87–91.

future expansion of the two electricity companies are subject to financial review conducted jointly by the Government and the companies. The two companies will make available the information on revenue and capital budgets as well as financial projections covering the preceding, current and at least four subsequent years. Estimated annual tariff adjustments required to meet the expansion plan should be spread evenly over the whole period. The results of are to be put to the Executive Council for approval.

In November and/or December each year, an audit and tariff review is conducted jointly by the Government and the two electricity companies. The companies provide all necessary documents to the Government concerning the estimated revenue required to meet their financial commitments (capital and operating costs) for the coming year. If the estimated average tariff is not higher than 0.8 cent per kWh above the current average tariff, and if it will not result in the company having excessive cash and bank balance, then tariff adjustment will be granted automatically.[3] The Government's approval for tariff increases should be sought if the increase is in excess of 0.8 cent per kWh. Apart from gaining the Government's approval, a new financial review should be conducted if the increase is in excess of 1.6 cents per kWh.

Thus, a number of automatic adjustment mechanisms in tariffs and returns are built into the Scheme of Control. These mechanisms reduce governance costs. In addition, the setting up of a development fund for making internal transfers helps stabilize returns and prices. Figure 4.2 shows the regulatory process under the Scheme of Control.

If a regulated company estimates revenue and cost correctly, and does not rely on the development fund to finance future expansion, the company will be able to earn the permitted returns without making any transfers from or to the development fund. An amount equal to 8% of the average of the opening and closing balances of the development fund will be transferred from the permitted return to the rate

---

3. Excessive cash and bank balance is defined as an amount which exceeds the gross tariff revenue for the last two months of the preceding year, see *The Schemes of Control* (Hong Kong Government 1982b), p. 81.

Figure 4.2   The Regulatory Process under the Scheme of Control

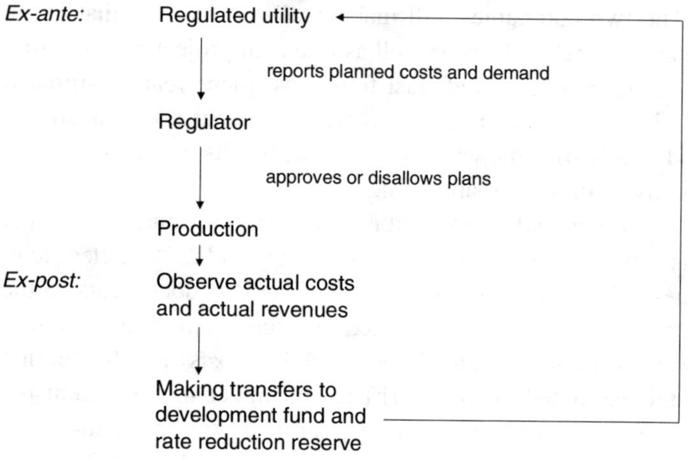

Ex-ante: Regulated utility ←─────────────────────────────┐

                         │
                         │ reports planned costs and demand
                         ↓

                    Regulator

                         │
                         │ approves or disallows plans
                         ↓

                    Production
                         │
                         ↓
Ex-post: Observe actual costs
                    and actual revenues

                         │
                         ↓

                    Making transfers to
                    development fund and ───────────────────────────┘
                    rate reduction reserve

reduction reserve. If the balance of the rate reduction reserve exceeds the total of the amount transferred for the current year and the three preceding years, it will be used to reduce tariffs by means of rebates, to consumers in the following year. Hence, as the development fund and the rate reduction reserve accumulate, the regulated firm has to reduce tariffs by rebates. CLP has argued that this would provide an incentive for the firm to minimize the amount of the development fund in order to reduce the interest payments (CLP 1964, p. 18).

In practice, however, since the realized revenues can be quite different from the estimated revenues, a regulated firm under the Scheme will have an incentive to overestimate revenue requirements so as to accumulate the development fund. In a later period, if the firm earns less than the permitted return, the deficiency will be compensated by a transfer from the development fund. In this way, the two electricity companies have an incentive to maintain a balance in the development fund sufficient to compensate any shortfall of net revenue below the permitted return. There are two ways of effecting the transfer:

(a) A transfer of cash/bank deposits from the development fund to compensate the shortfall, the cash being a distributable return to the shareholders as dividends;

(b) Debiting the development fund and crediting the shareholders' equity capital (i.e. shareholders' fund). The amount credited will not be distributed to the shareholders as dividends since it is not cash, it is a previous investment financed by the development fund.[4]

If the second method is used, then the existing shareholders of the company will enjoy a capital gain. These two methods of effecting transfers may have different financial implications. In the "Proposed Scheme of Control" laid out in the company's annual report, CLP provided examples to illustrate the operation of the Scheme of Control in periods of both ascending and descending development fund balances (CLP 1964).

In the Proposed Scheme, CLP also stated that with the terms governing the use of the development fund (including a charge on its average balance), "it was in the interest of the company to effect rate reductions and minimize the development fund." (p. 18) Also, CLP emphasized that permitted return was not guaranteed (p. 12).

4.2 Capital Structure and Cost of Capital

In this section, we analyze the interrelationship between the capital structure and the cost of capital under the Scheme of Control. We also consider the effects of the Scheme on the capital structure and the cost of capital of a regulated firm.

---

4. From a CLP letter dated 19 December 1991, the company informed the author that most of the development fund was used for acquiring fixed assets and that there was a very insignificant amount left as cash or deposits. This is not unexpected as the permitted rate of return (13.5%) on capital financed by the fund far exceeds the interest charge (8%). Using the fund to finance the acquisition of fixed assets is a much better alternative than depositing the money in the banks.

The asset value (A) of a firm is equal to its liabilities (L):

A = L.

To acquire its assets, a firm can basically rely on equity (E) and debt (D) financing:

L = E + D.

Hence, we have:

A = E + D.

In the case of the electricity companies in Hong Kong, there is an additional source of financing from the development fund (T):

A = E + D + T.

To simplify our analysis, we assume that there are no taxes. In fact, according to the accounting procedures discussed above, the permitted returns enjoyed by a firm under the Scheme of Control are based on after-tax profit, which is not subject to taxation. At present, the permitted rate on assets financed by equity is 15%, while the permitted rate on assets financed by the development fund is the same as that for debt-financed capital, both being fixed at 13.5%. If the assets of the electricity company are financed by equity, debt, and the development fund, the permitted return (PR) is obtained as follows:

PR = 15%E + 13.5%D + 13.5%T.

The net return (NR), that is permitted return less interest charges, is:

NR = (15%E + 13.5%D + 13.5%T) – 8%D – 8%T.

It should be noted that the maximum interest rate payable on long-term loans is 8% while the interest rate charged on the development fund is fixed at 8%.[5] Our illustration assumes both are fixed at 8%. The rate of return to equity capital (NR/E) is then:

---

5. The actual interest rates charged on loans made to CLP were between 7.25% and 8.5% (CLP 1979–1981).

NR/E = [(15%E + 13.5%D + 13.5%T) – 8%D – 8%T)]/E
= 15% + 5.5%[(D+T)/E].

From the above formula, if (D+T) = 0, the rate of return on equity is 15%. For example, if an all-equity firm has an asset of $100 and is earning a permitted return of $15 per year, then its rate of return on equity is 15% ($15/$100). The shareholders of the two regulated electric utilities can earn a rate of return on their equity capital above 15% if they finance part of their investment projects by debt and by the development fund, i.e. when (D+T) > 0. For example, suppose now the regulated firm issues debt, and has a debt-equity ratio of one. That means half of the firm's asset ($50) is financed by debt and the other half ($50) is financed by equity. Given that the interest rate paid on debt is 8%, the interest payment is $4. Applying the existing permitted rates on equity and debt to our example, the permitted return (PR) of the firm is:

PR = 15% × $50 + 13.5% × $50
= $14.25.

The net return (NR) is the permitted return after interest deductions, that is $10.25 (i.e. $14.25 – $4) in our simple example. The rate of return on equity (NR/E) now becomes 20.5% (i.e. $10.25/$50). Given a debt-equity ratio [(D+T)/E] of one, the rate of return on equity is 20.5%.

The permitted rate of return on equity is 15%. The shareholders of a regulated firm will compare this rate of return with the cost of equity capital to decide whether to invest or not. With regard to the cost of equity capital, we have different methods to compute it, the most notable one is the capital asset pricing model (CAPM).[6]

In the CAPM, the measure of market risk is known as beta (β). For example, the returns from an asset with a beta of 0.5 will fluctuate by 5% for each 10% fluctuation in the market's returns. It has been shown that the required risk premium for an asset is directly

---

6. The model was developed more or less simultaneously by Sharpe (1963; 1964), Lintner (1965), and Mossin (1966).

proportional to its beta. Therefore, the holder of an asset with a beta of 0.5 will require a risk premium only half as large as that offered by the market as a whole. If the market is efficient, the cost of equity capital will be equal to the expected rate of return.

The CAPM proposes that the current risk-return line is given by:

$$E(r_e) = r_f + \beta[E(r_m) - r_f],$$

where $E(r_e)$ = the expected rate of return for the regulated company's stock, r_f = the current risk-free rate of return, β = the stock's beta, $E(r_m)$ = the expected rate of return for the market, and $[E(r_m) - r_f]$ = risk premium.

If a regulated firm finances part of its investment by issuing debts, then we have to distinguish asset beta (β_A) from equity beta (β_E):

$$\beta_A = \beta_D (D/A) + \beta_E (E/A),$$

where β_D = debt beta. If $\beta_D = 0$, then we have:

$$\beta_A = \beta_E (E/A)$$
$$\beta_E = \beta_A (A/E)$$
$$\quad = \beta_A [(E+D)/E]$$
$$\quad = \beta_A [1 + (D/E)].$$

The effect of debt on the cost of equity capital is shown as follows:

$$r = [D/(D+E)] \times r_d + [E/(D+E)] \times r_e,$$

where r is the firm's overall cost of capital and r_d is the market return to debt (i.e. current interest rate). If a firm is financed in part by debt capital, then shareholders will bear a financial risk as well as a market risk. The finance theory argues that a higher debt-equity ratio will raise the equity beta of a firm, whilst leaving the firm's overall cost of capital unchanged. The finance theory also suggests that the overall cost of capital will not change if the firm changes its financial structure. Although the cost of debt capital is lower, the increase in debt raises the cost of equity capital, thus leaving the overall cost unchanged. The shareholders of a firm with a higher debt-equity ratio bear higher risk. Should the return of the firm decline, the rate of return on equity for a debt-financed company will decrease more sharply than that for an all-equity firm, as debtholders have prior claims on the firm's income. In other words, a higher debt-equity ratio raises the variability of returns. The implication is that firms with higher debt-equity ratios will have higher beta values because of the increased financial risk.

If the capital structure does not affect the firm's overall cost of capital, given r, financial risk will increase the cost of equity capital as shown below (by rearranging the above equation):

$$r_e = r + (r - r_d) \, D/E.$$

If $D = 0$, then $r_e = r$. If D is positive, $r_e > r$. Although debt financing increases the rate of return to shareholders, it also raises the cost of equity capital.

However, such an argument cannot be equally applied to the electricity companies which are subject to the Schemes of Control. The existence of a development fund stabilizes each company's returns, and hence higher debt need not increase the risk of equity capital. Suppose that a firm under the Scheme of Control has the following capital structure:

Equity: $50
Debt: $25
Development Fund: $25
(Total liability: $100, and total asset: $100)

The permitted return in this simple example is:

$15\% \times \$50 + 13.5\% \times \$50 = \$14.25$.

And the net return (return after interest) is:

$\$14.25 - 8\% \times \$50 = \$10.25$.

As mentioned above, financing by debt and by the development fund allows the firm to earn a rate of return on equity in excess of 15%. The rate of return on equity in this example is 20.5% (i.e. $10.25/$50). If the realized return is just $10, the deficiency ($4.25) can be compensated by a transfer from the development fund. This would allow the firm to earn the same permitted return (i.e. $14.25). After making the transfers, the new capital structure becomes:

Equity: $54.25
Debt: $25
Development fund: $20.75

Of course, there is a limit to drawing from the development fund. But so long as the development fund is sufficient to compensate any shortfalls in realized profits, the regulated firm is guaranteed to earn the permitted rate of return. Fluctuations in realized profit will not increase the risk borne by the shareholders. A direct testable implication then follows: a higher debt-equity ratio will increase the rate of return on equity, but it will not raise the financial risk or beta of a regulated company.

Our analysis does not imply that the beta value of a company under the Scheme of Control will be zero if the size of the development fund is sufficiently large. This is because in reality the Scheme regulates nominal returns, rather than real returns. The company still has to face fluctuations in real returns resulting from unanticipated inflation. In the United States, for example, several studies indicate that the rate-of-return regulation delays price adjustments during inflationary periods, resulting in diminished financial performance and increased systematic risk for regulated firms (Joskow and MacAvoy 1975, and Norton 1985).

4.3 Capital Structure and Input Choice

Under the Scheme of Control in Hong Kong, the permitted rate of return that a public utility can earn is fixed for a definite period of time. In the United States, however, the allowed rate can be adjusted in rate hearings. The principle allows public utilities to earn returns which cover the cost of capital. If a public utility wants the prices or the allowed rate to be changed, it should file a formal request, accompanied by submission of evidence in support of the request. As new prices will only be effective after the hearings, the regulated utility may earn more or less than the allowed rate. Hence, returns earned by regulated utilities can vary and are not "guaranteed". The situation is quite different in Hong Kong. As discussed earlier, the regulatory environment and the existence of development funds allow the two electricity utilities to earn the permitted rate of return for each and every year they have been subject to the Schemes of Control.

In U.S. regulatory hearings, the commission first determines the cost of equity capital (based on historical data) and then adds the cost of debt capital to work out the weighted average cost of capital. But in Hong Kong, as we have discussed, the permitted rate is basically imposed on fixed assets rather than on capital. The two regulated electricity companies are able to change the actual rate of return on equity by altering their debt-equity ratios.[7] By applying the Averch-Johnson Proposition, if the permitted rate of return is greater than the cost of capital, this will encourage the use of capital input and lead to a capital-bias expansion. By applying the same logic, unless the permitted rate, whether on equity or debt, is set equal to the expected cost of capital, there will be a distortion in the use of factors of production. In Chapter 6 we will consider whether the existing Scheme of Control arrangement has correctly set the permitted rates of return on equity and debt capital equal to their respective costs, and whether there is in fact any evidence of capital-bias expansion.

4.4 Development Fund and Productive Efficiency

It is often argued that if a regulated firm is allowed to set a price to recover all expenses, there will be a tendency for the firm to incur

---

7. We find a similar argument has been raised by Meyer (1976). In his model, he argued that when profit net of debt service is the objective, and the regulated firm can alter its capital structure, then the rate-of-return regulation does not necessarily imply the use of capital-bias and non-lease cost production methods. However, there is a major difference between our arguments. In Meyer's model, the allowed rate(s) can be influenced by the firm's capital structure; but in our model, we argue that both the permitted rate and the cost of capital can be influenced by the firm's capital structure.

wasteful expenditures. This is because if the regulator has imperfect information on the firm's cost function, and the firm is guaranteed a return which will recover any expenses, the firm may lack the incentive to minimize costs. The creation of the development fund, however, may mitigate this problem.

As shown in Figure 4.2, a regulated firm has to transfer all excess earnings to the development fund. When the development fund and rate reduction reserve accumulate to a certain level, the regulated firm has to make a price reduction. An unexpected reduction in production costs or an unexpected expansion in demand allows the firm to receive revenue in excess of its estimated production costs. As a result, the firm earns a return to capital in excess of the permitted return, and the development fund accumulates. A larger fund is then available for acquiring fixed assets so as to increase output, which allows the firm to earn a greater permitted return in later periods. On the contrary, an unexpected increase in the production cost or an unexpected contraction in demand depletes the development fund, putting pressure on the firm to reduce inefficiencies and providing a signal for the firm to contract capital acquisition or to disinvest.

It may be argued that because of fluctuations in demand and production costs, it is difficult for the regulator to determine whether higher costs are due to inefficiency, or due to a less favourable state of nature. Suppose that the firm behaves inefficiently and incurs wasteful expenditures. By asking for a tariff increase (which the Government grants), the regulated firm is not to be penalized in the current period as it can still earn a revenue covering all expenses (including wasteful expenses). However, under the Scheme of Control, the firm can request the same tariff increase by over-reporting expenses without incurring wasteful expenditures. The excess earnings earned afterwards are then transferred to the development fund, which may subsequently be drawn from when deficiencies arise. Unless the value derived from the waste exceeds the discounted value of the possible future deficiencies in returns, the regulated firm will not behave inefficiently. The regulated firm's incentive to over-expand is also curtailed as there is a limit to drawing on the fund to finance expansion.

Hence, the creation of a development fund not only maintains the stability of the regulatory system, but also provides some incentive for the regulated firm to achieve productive efficiency. However, as previously mentioned, there is a tendency for the regulated firm to over-report costs (and revenue requirements) so as to accumulate the development fund. Furthermore, once the regulated firm has accumulated a sufficient development fund to meet possible future deficiencies, the pressure on the firm to minimize costs would be reduced.

4.5 Concluding Remarks

Most of the models about the rate-of-return regulation assume a single allowed rate of return, without considering the effects of differential allowed rates for equity and debt capital. The effects of the rate-of-return regulation are then analyzed under the simple Averch-Johnson framework. Our analysis in this chapter, however, suggests that with differential permitted rates of return, there will be effects on the capital structure as well as on the input choice.

When the permitted rate of return on debt capital exceeds the interest costs, a regulated firm will tend to rely on debt capital. By increasing the debt-equity ratio, the actual rate of return on equity capital will increase. A higher debt-equity ratio does not necessarily increase the financial risk of the regulated firm, since the firm is protected by a long-term regulatory contract, and the development fund can help stabilize earnings. CLP argues that the Scheme of Control can facilitate low cost debt financing, but the company may not be sharing the benefits with its customers.

The conventional wisdom is that even if the regulator sets the permitted rate of return at a level equal to the cost of capital, the regulated firm will be indifferent between all feasible input combinations that meet the regulatory constraint because they all involve zero profit. However, if profits or excess earnings are to be transferred to a development fund, which will be drawn from later when the company is in an unfavourable state, then the regulated firm will have some incentive to attain *ex-post* productive efficiency. This incentive feature of the development fund has been ignored by those who argue for, or against, the existence of a development fund under the Scheme of Control. However, if the permitted rate of return on development fund capital is higher than its interest cost, there will be a different incentive for a regulated firm to accumulate the development fund. By over-charging, the regulated firm is able to borrow money from its customers at a relatively low interest cost and accumulate sufficient funds to meet possible future deficiencies. The regulatory system has put the burden on the regulator to discern such behaviour.

CHAPTER 5

Cost and Price Structures

Our discussion in Chapter 4 suggested that the Scheme of Control provides incentives for a regulated firm to lower costs and achieve productive efficiency. The benefits accrued can be shared between the regulated firm and the consumers. However, as the permitted rates of return on debt capital and development fund capital exceed the interest costs, a regulated firm under the Scheme may rely too much on debt capital to over-expand. This in turn would lead to higher electricity prices.

Many analysts would like to compare electricity prices in Hong Kong with those in other countries. Such a direct comparison is not very useful as electricity companies in other countries operate under different economic and regulatory environments. Population density and government taxes (or subsidies) also have a direct effect on electricity prices. Without taking these differences into account, one may draw the wrong conclusion from a simple tariff comparison between countries. As the population density in Hong Kong is high, we would normally expect a relatively lower cost (and price) of supplying electricity. Therefore, a more useful approach is to consider whether the customers in Hong Kong have paid more than necessary for their electricity bills. In this chapter, we analyze the cost and price structures of the two electricity companies in Hong Kong. Our focus is on whether there is any evidence of over-charging or over-expansion.

5.1 Vertical Structure of the Electricity Industry

Basically, we can divide the electricity industry into three stages: generation, transmission, and distribution.

Electricity is generated by applying mechanical energy to turn the shaft of a generator. A generator is a means of converting mechanical power into electric power. Generating plants are of three major types: steam, hydroelectric, and internal combustion. In steam-electric plants, water is heated to produce steam that drives a turbine connected to the unit's generator. Alternative fuels may be used to produce heat, the major ones being coal, oil, and natural gas. To secure fuel supply, some generating plants either provide their own fuels or enter into long-term contracts with fuel suppliers. Steam-electric generation may also come from nuclear plants, in which case, the heat is provided by a nuclear reactor. Hydroelectric plants are powered by falling water and have zero fuel costs. Internal combustion units (or gas turbines) have higher fuel costs but lower capital costs as compared with other alternatives. Recent technological development has improved the efficiency of gas-fired units. Many utilities (including CLP) around the world are turning towards building advanced combined-cycle units. These gas-fired units achieve the highest energy efficiency currently available, and the natural gas used in generation is also the cleanest fossil fuel available.

Electricity is transmitted from the generating plant to customers. It is transmitted at relatively low voltage from generating plants or a small number of connections to high-voltage transmission lines. Transmission consists of sending the electricity generated at the power stations through high voltage wires to substations, where it is transformed down to a low voltage ready for distribution through low-voltage lines to individual customers. It is possible to distinguish between the stages of distribution and supply of electricity. Distribution refers to the use of regional and local networks to distribute electricity while supply refers to the acquisition of electricity and its sale to customers.

It is generally agreed that the "transportation" services of transmission and distribution are characterized by natural monopoly cost conditions (Joskow and Schmalensee 1983, Vickers and Yarrow 1991a). However, the generation and supply of electricity to consumers are not naturally monopolistic, if they are separated from transmission. Lastly, it is not clear whether scale economies can be fully achieved by a vertically integrated firm in the generation, transmission, distribution, and supply of electricity.

5.2 Costs of Supplying Electricity

From our previous discussion, we may classify the costs of supplying electricity into two categories: capital costs and operating costs. Each category can be further divided into generation, transmission, distribution, and other costs.

According to conventional accounting procedures in the United States, generation accounts for about 50% of gross plant investment and 80% of annual operation and maintenance expenses.[1] The other 50% of gross plant investment is on transmission (15%) and distribution (35%) networks. Transmission expenses account for less than 2% of total operating and maintenance expenses.

Scale economies in generation might appear at the unit level, the plant level, or the firm level. For fossil-fuelled steam-electric generation, most observers seem to agree that some scale economies exist at the plant level, but opinions differ on how important they are. Most of the previous studies on scale economies in generation used the familiar Cobb-Douglas cost function and, more recently, the translog cost function.

In Joskow and Schmalensee's book (1983), a survey was made of previous studies pertaining to scale economies in the electric power industry. They concluded that on the generation side, at least two units are required for exploiting multi-unit economies. With 400 MW units required to exhaust unit-level economies, they obtained a rough estimate of 800 MW for minimum efficient plant capacity. At the firm level, Christensen and Greene's econometric study (1976) concluded, on the basis of 1970 data that economies of scale are fully exploited by utilities with about 4,000 MW of capacity, producing about 19

---

1. Joskow and Schmalensee (1983) provided a good discussion of the cost structure of the electricity industry. For detail, please refer to Joskow and Schmalensee 1983, pp. 45 and 62–63.

billion kWh per year. On the transmission side, a study by the Federal Energy Regulatory Commission (1981) suggested that a minimum of 10,000 MW of peak demand is required for exploiting the savings from an integrated transmission network.

Huettner and Landon (1978) conducted a study on the operating costs of supplying electricity in the United States, using 1971 data. They found that the average generation cost curve is U-shaped. The minimum point of the U-shaped average generation cost occurs at a firm size of 1,600 MW. The average transmission cost curve is an inverted U-shape, with the maximum point of this curve occurring at a capacity of 4,000 trillion MW. But the increase in the average transmission cost is extremely small, when capacity increases from 100 MW to 9,000 MW. Huettner and Landon also found that a higher proportion of large customers helps to reduce average transmission costs. Lastly, they found both the average distribution cost curve and the average administration and general cost curve to be somewhat L-shaped with minimum points occurring at about 2,500 MW. It was also found that higher consumption per customer reduces average administration and general costs.

There are several problems associated with these cost studies. In general, these studies use cross-section data, treating different firms as a single firm producing the same product. The assumption that different firms are operating under identical conditions is likely to produce errors. In fact, different firms have different production units and techniques, have different vintages of capital, and serve different customers. Moreover, these studies use accounting data, but different utilities may use different accounting rules. As a result, cost difference may simply reflect the differences in accounting practices. The use of time-series data of a single firm, though it has its own limitations, may overcome some of these problems.

5.3 Production Costs of CLP and HEC

(1) Capital Costs

By the end of 1992, the total generation capacity in Hong Kong was

9,037 MW (CLP: 6,432 MW, HEC: 2,605 MW). In 1993 and 1994, CLP's generation capacity increased to 7,540 MW when it commissioned production plants in China. These generating facilities constructed in China (at Daya Bay and Conghua) are not under the Scheme of Control. Needless to say, the rapid increase in generation capacity was accompanied by a corresponding increase in capital expenditure.

Soon after the Second World War, the two electricity companies reconstructed their plants (which had not been totally destroyed in the war). At the same time, they built new oil-fired generating units. The size of the units built before the 1970s was comparatively small and varied from 15 MW to 60 MW. In the 1970s, CLP, in operation with Esso, built 120 MW and 200 MW units on Tsing Yi Island, while HEC built 125 MW units on Ap Lei Chau Island. In the 1980s, in order to lessen Hong Kong's dependence on oil, the two companies engaged in the large scale construction of dual-fired generators (or coal-fired generators) which can fire both oil and coal. Large capital expenditures were incurred to cover the construction costs. CLP built four 350 MW units and four 677 MW units (total: 4,108 MW) at Castle Peak, while HEC built three 250 MW units and three 350 MW units (total: 1,800 MW) on Lamma Island. Some of HEC's dual-fired units were converted from oil-fired units relocated from Ap Lei Chau Island. The first dual-fired units of HEC and CLP were both commissioned in 1982. CLP completed the last 677 MW unit in 1990. Since the completion of these dual-fired units, CLP has turned the old oil-fired units into stand-by units in order to meet peak demands whilst HEC has converted the oil-fired units into gas turbines as stand-by units.

During the interim periods when the two companies were negotiating with the Government about the terms of the new Schemes of Control, both companies deferred their massive capital expenditures on new generation units. As mentioned earlier, HEC converted the old oil-fired units to meet increases in demand. Similarly, whilst CLP negotiated with the Government on the Scheme's new terms, the company constructed gas turbines which have lower capital costs but higher operating costs.[2] These two companies would commit to massive capital expenditure only after they had come into a new agreement with the Government.

The two companies' behaviour can be explained by the nature of the assets used in the electricity industry. The assets are specific, with little resale value. Once a company has committed to investing in these assets, a major part of the investment becomes a sunk cost. Apart from uncertainty over future demand, the company faces the risk of opportunistic behaviour on the part of the regulator. In order to assure adequate supply and, at the same time, not expose the company to high regulatory risk, building gas turbines during the interim period is a sensible solution.

Table 5.1 shows the generation units constructed by the two companies since the Second World War.

As shown in Table 5.1, the two companies built larger and larger power stations over time. Since 1966, CLP has relied on its associated companies (jointly owned by Exxon) to construct generating units, while it has mainly invested in transmission and distribution networks. Under the Scheme of Control, the two electricity companies are allowed to raise prices if they find that the expected revenue cannot cover the increased capital expenditures. This caused rapid increases in electricity prices in Hong Kong during the early 1980s. Once the Government has accepted the expansion plans submitted by the two companies, the permitted returns would be entirely based on their fixed assets. The two companies can adjust their tariffs automatically in order to achieve the permitted returns. No prudence test is imposed on them.

---

2. CLP adopted the strategy of building gas turbines to meet the growth in demand when the Scheme of Control was due to end. Before it renewed the contract with the Government in 1978, the company had purchased eight gas turbine units, totalling 504 MW in capacity, for commissioning between 1979 and 1981. Similarly, when the company negotiated with the Government again in 1991, it had started constructing a gas turbine power station at Penny's Bay, with a total capacity of 300 MW. The company also relied on the supply from the nuclear power station in China to meet anticipated growth in demand until 1995.

Table 5.1   Generation Units of CLP and HEC, 1947–1992

CLP, 1947–1966:
Hok Un A: Four 20 MW units
Hok Un B: Three 30 MW units
             Four 60 MW units
             One 20 MW gas turbine (commissioned in 1972)
             Total capacity: 430 MW

PEPCO (CLP's associated company), 1965–1977:
Hok Un C: Four 60 MW units
Tsing Yi A: Six 120 MW units
Tsing Yi B: Four 200 MW units
             One 42 MW gas turbine
             Total capacity: 1,802 MW

KESCO (CLP's associated company), 1978–1992:
Hok Un C: One 56 MW gas turbine
             Three gas turbines totalled 208 MW
Castle Peak A: Four 60 MW gas turbines
             Four 350 MW dual-fired units
             Total capacity: 1,904 MW
Penny's Bay: Three 100 MW gas turbines

CAPCO (CLP's associated company), 1981–1992:

Castle Peak B: Four 677 MW dual-fired units
             Total capacity: 2,708 MW

HEC:
North Point: Two 15 MW units
(1947–1966)   One 20 MW unit
             Five 30 MW units
             Two 60 MW units
             Total capacity: 320 MW

Ap Lei Chau: Two 60 MW units
(1967–1981)   Seven 125 MW units
             One 11 MW gas turbine
             Total capacity: 1,006 MW

Lamma Island: Three 250 MW dual-fired units
(1982–1992)   Three 350 MW dual-fired units
             Total capacity: 1,800 MW

Sources: Annual reports of CLP, 1947–1992, and annual reports of HEC, 1955–
           1992.

The system is entirely different from the "used and useful" standard adopted by the regulatory commissions in the United States. In U.S. public hearings, electric utilities are required to pass the prudence test. Their allowed returns are only based on the capital assets which are prudently made, are used and are useful for electricity production. In Hong Kong, the regulator is burdened with having to grant expansion plans which will neither lead to electricity shortage nor excessive capital investment. As the regulator is averse to political risk, he might try to avoid the risk of refusing expansion plans which might eventually cause electricity shortage. As a result, the existing Scheme of Control inevitably produces excess capacity.

The Scheme of Control has also caused the early retirement of generating facilities. The expected useful lives of some fixed assets have been set too low. For example, the expected useful life of a generating plant and its machinery was once fixed at 20 years, but the actual useful live of this asset should normally exceed 30 years. The resulting higher rate of depreciation has increased accounting costs and led to higher tariffs. The generating facilities installed at Ap Lei Chau by HEC during the 1970s were all decommissioned prior to 1989. Some of the generating units had only been in use for less than ten years. After relocating the generating facilities to Lamma Island, HEC converted the vacant site into a private residential estate (South Horizons). In the early 1990s, CLP decommissioned generating facilities at Hok Un and Tsing Yi which had been installed in the 1970s. The Government has approved CLP to decommission some operational power stations at Tsing Yi several years ahead of schedule. The vacant site at Hok Un will also be redeveloped into a housing estate. The decision on the early decommissioning of these facilities may only be one which serves the company's interest, rather than the consumer's interest.[3]

---

3. The Government was not unaware of this problem. In the 1988 review of the Scheme of Control Agreement, the useful lives of certain assets were revised upwards. In the new Schemes, signed in the early 1990s, the useful life of a generating plant and its machinery was revised upwards to 25–30 years.

CLP's annual reports provide detailed capital expenditures on generation, transmission and distribution (see Table 5.2). HEC's annual reports, however, only provide figures on total capital expenditure.

As we can see from Table 5.2, both CLP's and HEC's capital expenditures increased rapidly after the signing of their Schemes of Control in 1978. The increases can be explained by the construction of dual-fired generators which would subsequently save operating costs such as fuel and labour. However, whether the reduction in

Table 5.2 Capital Expenditure of CLP and HEC, 1947–1990

1. CLP's Capital Expenditure on Generation

Period	Nominal capital expenditure	Real capital expenditure*	Generating capacity	Real capacity cost per MW
1965–1977	HK$1,163 m	HK$836 m	1,802 MW	HK$0.46 m
1978–1986	HK$6,306 m	HK$2,012 m	1,904 MW	HK$1.06 m
1981–1990	HK$13,420 m	HK$3,024 m	2,708 MW	HK$1.12 m

2. CLP's Capital Expenditure on Transmission and Distribution

Period	Nominal capital expenditure	Real capital expenditure*	Increase in capacity	Real capacity cost per MW
1966–1978	HK$1,511 m	HK$979 m	1,790 MW	HK$0.55 m
1979–1990	HK$14,985 m	HK$3,330 m	3,980 MW	HK$0.84 m

3. Total Capital Expenditure

Period		Real capital expenditure*	Increase in capacity	Real capacity cost per MW
1947–1963	CLP:	HK$428 m	272 MW	HK$1.57 m
	HEC:	HK$292 m	156 MW	HK$1.87 m
1964–1978	CLP:	HK$2,056 m	1,850 MW	HK$1.11 m
	HEC:	HK$1,095 m	735 MW	HK$1.49 m
1979–1990	CLP:	HK$8,415 m	3,980 MW	HK$2.11 m
	HEC:	HK$3,927 m	1,325 MW	HK$2.96 m

Note: *Real capital expenditure is measured by 1964 prices.
Sources: Annual reports of CLP, 1947–1992, and annual reports of HEC, 1955–1992. Hong Kong Government, Electricity Supply Companies Commission 1959.

operating costs can justify the rapid capital expansion is an empirical matter. It is possible that overall costs might actually have increased. Before 1978, capital cost on generation accounted for about 50% of total capital cost; but after 1978, its share increased steadily to about 60%. CLP has a much lower capacity cost than HEC, which could perhaps be explained by the scale effect. However, both companies' unit capacity costs in real terms doubled after 1978.

(2) Operating Costs

CLP's annual reports provide detailed figures of separate operating expenses for the period 1967–1977 (see Table 5.3). But for other years, the reports only provide total fuel costs and total operating expenses. As shown in Table 5.3, the cost of generation, which accounts for 80 to 90% of total operating expenses (excluding depreciation), is the major component of operating expenses. Of the generation cost, fuel costs account for about 70% in 1977. Other operating expenses are basically wages. These figures are consistent with other studies.

Table 5.3 Nominal Operating Expenses of CLP, 1967–1977 (in HK$ million)

Year	Generation (fuel)	Transmission & distribution	Administration & general	Tariffs (cents/kWh) Bulk	Tariffs (cents/kWh) Other
1967	130 (69)	10	18	7.4	17.2
1968	152 (80)	13	18	7.5	17.1
1969	182 (91)	16	21	7.4	16.4
1970	213 (104)	19	26	8.0	15.2
1971	261 (130)	20	36	8.8	16.0
1972	283 (135)	22	38	8.8	16.0
1973	291 (121)	23	47	8.1	15.3
1974	512 (323)	24	54	13.2	20.5
1975	672 (459)	25	55	16.5	23.7
1976	757 (529)	27	50	16.7	23.9
1977	838 (601)	31	65	16.8	23.9

Source: Annual reports of CLP, 1967–1977.

Table 5.3 also shows CLP charges a much lower average price for bulk industrial users. It was found that the average prices during this period just covered the average generation expenses, leaving little for recovering other capital and operating expenses. Most previous studies suggest that generation costs do not vary with per person consumption. In other words, average generation costs are more or less the same for large and small customers. Therefore, it seems that CLP tried to recover the capital costs entirely from smaller users.

If industrial users contributed to the peak load of CLP, then the pricing strategy adopted by CLP is just the opposite of the peak-load pricing arrangement suggested by some economists (see Steiner 1957). These economists argue that peak-load users should bear the capacity cost. In fact, CLP admitted that the company had a policy of subsidizing industry. This subsidizing policy can partly explain why CLP has a much larger proportion of industrial customers than HEC (e.g. in 1976, CLP: 49%, HEC: 15%). The price differential between bulk users and other users decreased in the 1980s. Coupled with the structural change of the Hong Kong economy (from manufacturing to services industries), the proportion of industrial users of CLP decreased steadily throughout the 1980s.

The number of workers working in electricity companies increased over time, and reached a maximum in the early 1980s. The number decreased up until 1988 but has increased again in recent years.[4] The reduction in labour costs and the reduction in fuel costs upon the completion of dual-fired units, have caused the operating costs to decrease (in real terms) steadily throughout the 1980s. These reductions indicate that a substantial factor substitution was under way in the electricity industry. Fuel and labour were replaced by capital. Is such a factor substitution beneficial to consumers or is it just a direct result from the Averch-Johnson proposition that the rate-of-return regulation leads to capital bias? The answers may come from further empirical studies.

---

4. In 1994, the workforce of CLP decreased by about 300 because of the company's reorganization.

5.4 Tariff Structures of CLP and HEC

(1) The Tariff History

After the Second World War and into the 1950s, the tariff structures of the two electricity companies were divided into lighting, power, special heating, and bulk supply. In the early 1950s, both companies introduced a surcharge, which was purported to cover the large increase in the price of fuel due to the termination of the fixed price fuel contracts (Hong Kong Government, Electricity Supply Companies Commission 1959, p. 17). It was also this fuel surcharge which caused public discontent and led the Government to appoint an Electricity Supply Companies Commission in 1959. The Commission was asked to consider the form and the extent of control imposed on the two companies. In November 1964, CLP, in cooperation with Esso, signed a Scheme of Control Agreement with the Government. CLP promised to reduce its tariffs in the coming years. Consumers also benefited from discounts or rebates resulting from the setting up of the rate reduction reserve. Hence, it was expected that the Scheme of Control would reduce the average price charged by CLP, at least for the first few years after the signing of the Scheme.

In June 1969, CLP published a new tariff system comprising a general tariff for ordinary consumers and a bulk tariff for large consumers. According to CLP, under the new system, the average charge for electricity would be further reduced. Rapid increases in production costs as a result of the oil crisis caused an increase in basic tariffs in April 1974, this being the first increase since CLP was subject to government control. Basic tariffs remained unchanged until January 1980.

The two electricity companies in Hong Kong have adopted similar pricing policies since the mid-1960s. Basically, separate price structures are applied both to small users (mainly domestic and commercial users) and to large users (mainly industrial users). Prices are lower for the latter group.

Both companies adopted declining-block (or multiple block) price structures.[5] For smaller users, the declining-block pricing structure consists of a minimum initial charge and a per kilowatt-hour (kWh) charge that falls in blocks as consumption increases. For large users, on the other hand, the declining-block structure consists of a demand charge and an energy charge. The demand charge is a function of kilowatts which measures the demand for capacity, not kilowatt-hours, which measure use.

In 1983, CLP introduced a new pricing arrangement called the Domestic Night Storage Water Heating Rate. Under this arrangement, a much lower rate is applied to the use of electricity for domestic electricity storage water heaters during the off-peak period, from 2300 hours to 0700 hours. Apart from this arrangement, there is no similar time-of-day (peak-load) pricing adopted by the two companies. Lastly, all prices are subject to the same fuel clause adjustment.

In the Electricity Supply Companies Commission's report (1959), CLP admitted that the company had a policy of subsidizing industries. The following shows the relative (average) price between general and bulk tariffs (for HEC, it is between non-industrial and industrial tariffs):

Year	CLP	HEC
1962	2.36	N.A.
1967	2.28	1.31
1975	1.43	1.16
1981	1.17	N.A.

Obviously, CLP charged a much lower price to bulk industrial users as compared with general domestic and commercial users in the 1960s. In the early 1980s, CLP increased the prices charged to bulk users substantially, which reduced the price differential between bulk users and other users. Although industrialists strongly protested CLP's new rate policy, the Government accepted CLP's new policy. Therefore, it seems that the subsidizing policy came to an end in the early 1980s.

---

5. To induce energy conservation, the Government has recently prompted the two electricity companies to revise their declining-block price structures and to introduce pricing policies which encourage conservation.

In the 1980s, in order to lessen Hong Kong's dependence on oil, the two electricity companies engaged in the large scale construction of dual generators (or coal-fired generators) which can fire both oil and coal. A substantial capital expenditure was required to meet the construction costs. This, coupled with rapid oil price increases, caused the two companies to increase tariffs sharply in the late 1970s and early 1980s. From 1987 to 1991, the basic tariffs charged by CLP remained more or less unchanged whereas HEC continued to increase basic tariffs each year. Although the use of coal in electricity generation can reduce fuel cost, there is additional capital expenditure in building coal-fired generators. The overall impact of building coal-fired generators on production cost and price of electricity is not clear.

Figure 5.1 and Figure 5.2 show the nominal average prices and real average prices (based on 1964 prices) of electricity charged by

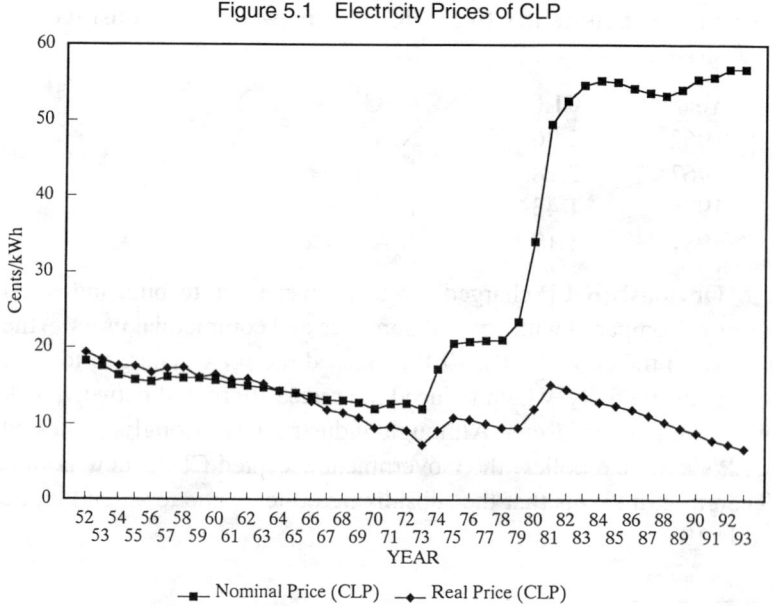

Figure 5.1   Electricity Prices of CLP

Sources: Annual reports of CLP, 1952–1993. Hong Kong Government, Electricity Supply Companies Commission 1959.

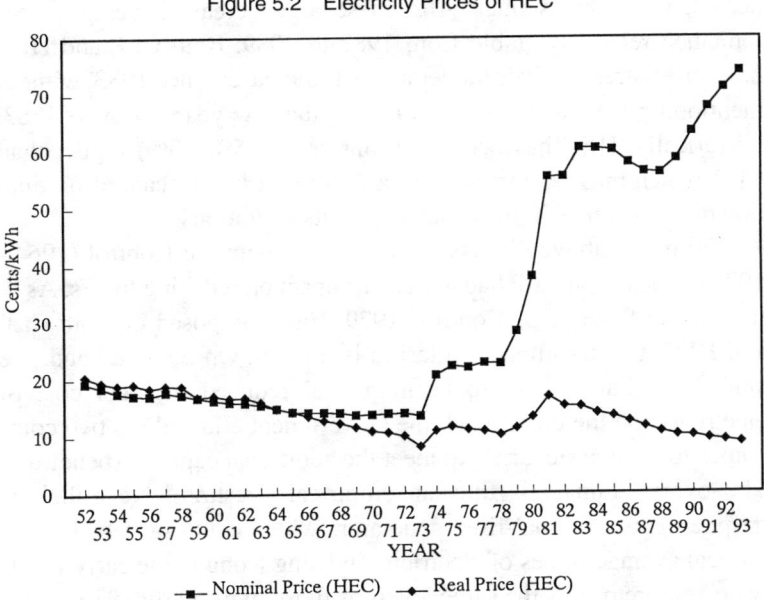

Figure 5.2 Electricity Prices of HEC

Sources: Annual reports of HEC, 1955–1993. Hong Kong Government, Electricity
Supply Companies Commissin, 1959.

CLP and HEC respectively from 1952 to 1993. We can divide the
tariff history of the two companies into three periods: (1) 1952–1963,
(2) 1964–1978, and (3) 1979–1993. From 1952 to 1963, both companies' nominal prices decreased steadily. The downward trend in
tariffs continued during the early years of the second period. In 1974,
both companies raised prices drastically, as a result of the first oil
crisis. Prices then remained stable from 1975 to 1978.

CLP renewed its Scheme of Control agreement with the Government in late 1978 and HEC formally entered into the Scheme in 1979.
After entering into the Scheme, HEC raised its tariffs significantly.
The tariff increases were partly due to the second oil crisis and partly
due to the rapid capital expenditure required to finance construction
of coal-fired generators. CLP also raised prices during the same

period, but not by as much. After these large increases, average prices remained relatively stable from 1982 to 1989. Both CLP and HEC have often stressed their moderate tariff increases since 1983, without mentioning the rapid increases during the few years prior to 1983. Historically, HEC has been charging prices (5%–20%) higher than CLP, which may be attributed to a difference in the scale of production or a difference in the efficiency of its operations.

From the above discussion, the first Scheme of Control (1964–1978) imposed on CLP had a greater impact on reducing tariffs. As to the second Scheme of Control (1979–1993), imposed on both CLP and HEC, the net impact on tariffs is unclear. On the one hand, the shift from burning oil to burning coal reduced the fuel cost of electricity; on the other hand, the Government allowed the two companies to raise basic tariffs to meet the additional capital expenditure. The overall impact is thus an empirical question.[6] Nevertheless, despite the use of coal-fired generators which could save fuel costs, the real average prices of electricity in Hong Kong in the early 1990s were at more or less the same levels as those in the early 1970s.

As shown in Figure 5.1 and Figure 5.2, electricity prices in Hong Kong fluctuated widely. The construction of coal-fired generators and increases in oil price during the early 1980s increased prices sharply. But once the oil-fired generators had been commissioned, the two electricity companies were able to lower prices due to the decrease in fuel cost. Wide fluctuations in electricity prices in Hong Kong are the result of electric utilities being able to raise prices whenever costs rise.

5.5 Concluding Remarks

Studies in the United States suggest that the scale effect is an important factor affecting production costs in the electricity industry. The

---

6. The author has formulated some econometric models to test the effect of the Scheme of Control on electricity prices. Results suggest that the first Scheme had a greater effect on reducing prices than did the second Scheme.

scale effect is greater for capital cost than for operating cost and it is greater in transmission and distribution than in generation and supply. Economies of scale are not crucial in the generation and supply businesses. Comparing the capital costs of the two electricity companies in Hong Kong also indicates that potential capital cost saving is enormous if the two companies integrate their transmission and distribution networks. Prices charged by CLP are now lower than those of HEC. As the two companies' fuel costs and operating costs should not differ substantially, the lower price charged by CLP is basically due to its lower capacity costs, particularly in terms of transmission and distribution. It is expected that if both companies share the same transmission and distribution network, substantial scale economies could be achieved. Reserve capacity for meeting contingencies could also be reduced significantly.

It has been shown that the Scheme of Control had a greater effect on reducing electricity prices in the 1960s and 1970s. The price effect in the 1980s was smaller because of the rapid capital expansion. Once the two companies entered into a new Scheme of Control with the Government in 1978, they increased capital expenditure rapidly. It seems that the regulator in Hong Kong has done nothing to prevent this. Although the two companies have to submit financial plans to the Government to justify their demand forecasts and capital expansion, there is no mechanism in the existing Scheme to reward correct estimates or to penalize any over-estimates of future demand. There is a problem of asymmetric information, the companies have some private information not known by the regulator. As shown in Table 5.4, the expansion in capacity is often many years ahead of the system's maximum demand level. In the past, CLP might expand more than necessary in order to meet the higher maximum demand due to the export of electricity to China (see Table 5.4). The recent decrease in CLP's export of electricity to China means that users in Hong Kong have to pay a price for the company's previous rapid expansion.

Although it is often difficult to distinguish between higher reliability and wasteful excess capacity, the excess of installed capacity above the system's maximum, as shown in Table 5.4, cannot

Table 5.4 Installed Capacity and System Maximum Demand,
1981–1994 (in MW)

Year	CLP*		HEC	
	Capacity	Maximum demand	Capacity	Maximum demand
1981	2,656	2,109 (2,109)	1,060	852
1982	3,006	2,269 (2,280)	1,435	932
1983	3,356	2,475 (2,538)	1,560	1,012
1984	3,664	2,652 (2,710)	1,685	1,064
1985	3,924	2,835 (2,987)	1,685	1,150
1986	4,361	3,123 (3,355)	1,685	1,259
1987	4,778	3,440 (3,670)	1,915	1,379
1988	5,455	3,593 (3,849)	2,005	1,421
1989	5,455	3,892 (4,202)	2,005	1,540
1990	6,132	4,058 (4,407)	2,255	1,613
1991	6,132	4,180 (4,828)	2,255	1,680
1992	6,432	4,365 (5,289)	2,605	1,819
1993	6,430	4,432 (5,244)	2,605	1,890
1994	7,540	4,730 (5,948)	2,605	2,021

Note: * Figures which include demand from China are in parentheses.
Sources: Annual reports of CLP, 1981–1994, and annual reports of HEC, 1981–
1994.

be justified by any international standard of maintaining the system's reliability and reducing outages.[7] As permitted returns are based on fixed assets, it follows that consumers have to pay higher prices for unwanted excess capacity. As a matter of fact, regulators in Hong Kong have, from time to time, admitted that the main objective of the Scheme of Control arrangement is to encourage privately-owned utilities to make investments. However, such an arrangement has also rewarded excessive investment. Under the existing Scheme of

7. In 1992, CLP had an excess capacity (over local maximum demand) of 47.4%, while the figure for HEC was 43.2%. The common standard of excess capacity to ensure reliable supply is 25%. As the demand from China dropped sharply in 1994, the problem of excess capacity of CLP became obvious and aroused public concern in early 1995. In 1995, both CLP and HEC have an excess capacity of about 46%.

Control, the two electricity companies are allowed to raise prices to meet capacity expansion. The Scheme of Control has put the burden on the regulator to approve or disallow expansion plans submitted by the regulated utilities.

In addition, there is a lack of incentive for the two companies to adopt demand-side management or peak-hour pricing. If customers were successfully encouraged to shift their demand for electricity to off-peak hours, the demand for additional generating facilities would decrease. Consequently, the asset base would become smaller and this would lower the permitted return of a regulated firm.

It may be argued that the figures shown in Table 5.4 are realized figures. It may be the case that, *ex-post*, demand falls short of the *ex-ante* level, and therefore the two companies should not be punished for an unanticipated fall in demand. But it is difficult to distinguish between incorrect forecasts made unintentionally and those made intentionally. What is needed is a self-revelation mechanism to encourage truthful forecasting. The two companies should be treated like other firms in the market, that is to say, they should have to bear the financial consequences of their demand forecasts.

Lastly, if the permitted rate of return is set at a level reflecting the cost of capital, then a regulated company will have less incentive to increase capital excessively. This is because the company will earn a rate of return which can only cover the opportunity cost of the investment fund. Investing in other alternatives is equally profitable. Hence, our next task is to measure the cost of capital in the electricity industry and then to compare it with the permitted rate. The problem with the Scheme of Control will become clearer after we have considered the concept of the cost of capital in Chapter 6.

CHAPTER 6

Cost of Capital Analysis

This chapter is a study of the cost of capital and the capital structure of a firm under the Scheme of Control. In the first section, we discuss the cost of capital concept and its importance in the regulation of public utilities. While the cost of capital concept is widely used in the regulatory process in the United States and the United Kingdom, the concept seems to be unfamiliar to the regulator in Hong Kong.[1] In this chapter, we provide a comparative analysis of the cost of capital estimation. Three major methods will be evaluated: (1) the comparative earnings method, (2) the dividend growth model, and (3) the capital asset pricing model. Recent data on the two regulated electricity companies (CLP and HEC) will be used to measure their costs of capital. Throughout the analysis, we use the Hong Kong and China Gas Company Limited (HKG), which is an unregulated town gas company, and other listed companies under the Scheme of Control as examples for making comparisons.

In this chapter, our focus is on the capital asset pricing model in measuring the cost of capital. We try to examine the effect of capital structure on the capital cost of a firm under the Scheme of Control. The chapter closes with a comparative study of permitted returns and costs of capital for different regulated companies subject to the Scheme of Control. Beta values of various regulated industries in the United States and the United Kingdom are also examined. Our aim in

---

1. In late 1994, the Finance Branch of the Government completed a report named *Review on Government Utilities*. In the report, the Government started to recognize the importance of using the concept of cost of capital in determining target returns of government utilities.

this chapter is to highlight the various problems associated with the Scheme of Control in setting the permitted rates of return.

6.1 Cost of Capital Concept

At the very beginning of *The Schemes of Control* (Hong Kong Government 1982b), it is stated clearly that the Government recognizes that the regulated companies and their shareholders are entitled to earn a return which is reasonable in relation to the risks involved and the capital invested and retained in the business. In return, the Government must be assured that service to the public is adequate, efficient and of high quality, and is provided at the lowest cost (p. 5). To protect the producer's right to serve, the Government faces a crucial problem: "What constitutes a reasonable return?"

It is generally accepted that in order to provide incentives for future investments, a public utility should be able to earn a return which covers its cost of capital. The cost of capital is a forward-looking and is essentially an application of the concept of opportunity cost. As future returns are uncertain, the cost of capital is an expected rate of return which depends on the risk involved in the investment. Investors also face alternative investment opportunities, so the expected return must be sufficient to compensate investors for the forgone return in alternative investment opportunities. The U.S. Supreme Court has established that utilities under the rate-of-return regulation must be allowed an opportunity to earn returns sufficient to attract capital and be comparable to expected returns in other industries of equivalent risk. In the Hope Natural Gas case, the court clearly stated that:

> The rate-making process under the act, i.e. the fixing of "just and reasonable" rates, involves a balancing of the investor and the consumer interests ... From the investor or company point of view it is important that there be enough revenue not only for operating expenses but also for the capital costs of the business ... By that standard the return to the equity owner should be commensurate with returns on investments in other enterprises having corresponding risks. That return, moreover, should be sufficient to assure

confidence in the financial integrity of the enterprise, so as to maintain its credit and to attract capital.[2]

The Hope case emphasizes the importance of commensurate returns and the attraction of capital. According to economic theory, if the regulator sets the permitted rate of return below the cost of capital, managers of the regulated companies will be unwilling to increase their production capacity. While existing customers may benefit from this policy, future customers are likely to lose. If the amount of investment in the electricity industry is not adequate, customers will face inefficient (e.g. higher fuel costs), insufficient supplies, and consequently, higher prices and more service outages.

Conversely, if the regulator sets the permitted rate above the cost of capital, stockholders of the regulated companies will earn more than they would in comparable-risk investments in the market. As a result, customers will be forced to pay a higher price for the services. This will cause excessive capital to be invested by the regulated companies. Thus, even for a public utility, its cost of capital should be determined by the financial markets, not by its regulator.

In practice, however, it is difficult to measure the cost of capital and then set the permitted rate of return accordingly. Two important problems have to be solved in any rate-making process. First, there is a problem of measuring risk. As the cost of capital reflects the returns on investment of equivalent risk, we have to select a method of measuring the degrees of risk associated with different investment opportunities. Since risk is a theoretical concept which is not observable, our measurements are by proxy. Second, there is a problem of measuring capital. An accounting concept of capital is different from an economic concept of capital. Considerable effort has been spent on examining the question of what constitutes the rate base for regulated utilities. Some regulatory agencies use original cost as the rate base, others use reproduction cost (which is higher than the original cost in

---

2. *Federal Power Commission* v. *Hope Natural Gas Company*, 320 U.S. 590 at 603.

a period of inflation), and still others use "fair value", which is somewhere between original cost and reproduction cost.

Theoretically, the value of the rate base may be determined independently of the permitted rate of return but empirical evidence in the United States has suggested that the permitted rate of return depends on the selection of the rate base. In a landmark study, Eiteman (1962) found that firms under original cost jurisdiction had been granted the highest permitted rates of return and firms operating in reproduction cost jurisdiction had been permitted the lowest. The lower permitted rate partially offsets the larger rate base. Other studies (e.g. Primeaux 1978; Nelson and Primeaux 1984) have reached a similar conclusion: there is no statistical difference in earnings of firms regulated by original cost, fair value, and reproduction cost jurisdictions. Hence, we have to consider the permitted rate of return together with the rate base valuation. Failure to do so would affect our conclusion of whether the permitted rate reflects the cost of capital.

It has been argued that for the sake of fairness, the permitted rate of return should be equal to the cost of capital. Unfortunately, there is not a simple way to define what a fair return is. Setting the permitted rate equal to the cost of capital is only one definition of fairness. There are other definitions of fairness. One notion is that even though the permitted rate is not equal to the cost of capital, the return could still be fair provided that all contracting parties, including regulators, investors and customers, understood in advance that this was a condition of the contract.

Greenwald (1984) investigated the notion of fairness of any rate base valuation rule. Capital invested in the electricity industry is specific and has significantly lower value in alternative uses. This may create an incentive for the regulators to behave opportunistically and to appropriate the quasi-rent of the electric utilities through policy changes. If investors anticipate this incentive problem, they will respond by reducing investment. In the extreme case, the "equilibrium" solution to this problem will involve no long-lived investment at all which will make all parties worse off. According to Greenwald (1984), this dynamic consistency or credibility problem can be solved by a commitment made by the regulators:

Restricting regulators with an appropriate "fairness" criterion may, therefore, be essential to establish the viability of the originally optimal equilibrium. The simplest way to do this would be to require by law that past regulatory promises be honoured in future proceedings. To maintain the flexibility of regulators to respond to unforseen circumstances, however, the set of legally binding past promises should be minimally constraining. Since investors should be concerned only with future returns, the minimum acceptable set of legal constraints need only guarantee the value of future income implied by past promises (Greenwald 1984, p. 86).

Greenwald argued that there is nothing inherently fair about any rate base valuation rule, fairness merely implies that regulators behave consistently regarding the risks they impose on investors. A regulatory scheme is fair to investors if and only if the market value in the future fulfils the market value promises made when the contract was signed. From this viewpoint, a long-term contract between a regulated firm and the Government serves to avoid the above dynamic consistency problem. Once the two parties have agreed on the terms stipulated in the contract (including the permitted rate of return and the rate base valuation method), they will commit to honour the contract. Investors of the regulated firm will expect to earn the permitted return and the regulators are restricted not to behave opportunistically. Such a contract can be considered fair to both investors and customers, provided that the permitted rate does not include excess earnings or that the promised initial market value of the firm is set at zero (i.e. the firm earns a return just sufficient to cover its cost).

Having discussed the cost of capital concept and its importance in the rate-making process, we proceed to consider the common methods used to measure the cost of capital.

6.2 Methods of Estimating the Cost of Capital

(1) The Comparative Earnings (CE) Method

Traditionally, the comparative earnings (CE) method is the most widely used and accepted approach. It starts by selecting a sample of firms believed to be of comparable risk in their operations, and then calculates each's return on equity (ROE), which is simply the ratio of book earnings to the book value of equity. The cost of capital for a regulated utility is then inferred from the book rates of these comparable-risk companies.

This method rests on a basic assumption: equating the book rates of return of comparable-risk companies and the regulated company can assure that the latter earns its cost of capital. But if the rates of return earned by unregulated companies are above their costs of capital, this will lead to an incorrect estimate. Table 6.1 shows the book rates of return of the three power companies in Hong Kong.

In Table 6.1, we can see that both regulated utilities are earning less than the unregulated one in the late 1980s. After the publication of the *Report on the Safety and Legal Aspects of Both Town Gas and LPG Operations in Hong Kong* (British Gas Corporation

Table 6.1 Book Rates of Return, 1981–1992*

Year	CLP	HEC	HKG
1981	18.9%	16.6%	10.1%
1982	21.3%	18.4%	14.9%
1983	22.5%	20.0%	19.1%
1984	23.8%	13.0%	22.4%
1985	25.5%	22.7%	16.9%
1986	25.1%	21.2%	18.4%
1987	24.4%	19.2%	22.5%
1988	23.3%	22.7%	25.7%
1989	22.7%	23.7%	27.6%
1990	23.2%	24.4%	28.3%
1991	24.9%	26.5%	28.7%
1992	24.7%	29.8%	29.2%
Average:	23.4%	21.5% (24.4%)**	22.0%

Notes: * Figures after 1992 are not shown as HKG revaluated its assets in 1993. End-of-year equity is used. Profits after tax and Scheme of Control adjustments are used in our calculations.
         ** For period after Group reorganization in 1987.
Sources: Annual reports of CLP, HEC, and HKG, 1981–1992.

International Service 1981), the Government introduced a piped gas policy in order to discourage the use of gas cylinders. Since then, the business of HKG expanded rapidly and its book rate of return increased to 28.7% in 1992. Recently, HKG was accused of earning "excessive" profit by the public and government regulation has been called for.[3] The Government refused to regulate the company based on the argument that substitutes, such as liquefied petroleum gas (LPG), are available for consumers to choose. Therefore, if HKG is earning monopoly profit, then its book rate of return is a poor estimate of the costs of capital of the two regulated firms.

Returning to the two electricity companies, HEC has engaged itself again in property development in recent years. As a result of the property boom in the early 1990s, the performance of the company improved greatly. The book rate of return of the company increased from 19.2% in 1987 to 29.8% in 1992. For CLP, the proportion of its profits from sources other than the Scheme of Control has also increased over time. CLP has also begun to redevelop its previous plant sites into residential estates, and the effect on the company's book rate of return will become apparent in the coming few years. But as the two companies did not provide separate accounts clearly, we are unable to determine the exact equity returns on regulated and non-regulated businesses.

In Table 6.2, we compare the rates of return on equity of the two electricity companies over time. Our aim is to evaluate the effect of the Scheme of Control on the actual equity rate of return of the two companies. Before the setting up of the Electricity Supply Companies Commission in 1959, the real rates of return of the two companies exceeded 22%. These attractive rates of return invited government control. Once the first Scheme of Control was introduced, the companies' real rates of return decreased significantly to below 10%.

---

3. A preliminary consultancy report published by the Consumer Council in Hong Kong highlighted that HKG earned an average rate of return on assets of 26% for the period 1987–1991, which was far above the rates of return earned by utilities in Western countries (see *Ming Pao*, 1 November 1993). The full report was published in 1995 (see Consumer Council 1995).

Table 6.2 Rates of Return on Equity*

Period		CLP	HEC
1946–1958	Nominal rate of return	25.7%	23.7%
	Inflation rate	1.0%	1.0%
	Real rate of return	24.7%	22.7%
1964–1978	Nominal rate of return	15.0%	15.5%
(First Scheme)	Inflation rate	5.8%	5.8%
	Real rate of return	9.2%	9.7%
1979–1992	Nominal rate of return	22.4%	20.5%
(Second Scheme)	Inflation rate	9.4%	9.4%
	Real rate of return	13.0%	11.1%

Notes: * End-of-year equity is used.
          Profits after tax and Scheme of Control adjustments are used in our
          calculations.
Sources: Hong Kong Government, Electricity Supply Companies Commission
          1959. Annual reports of HEC, CLP, 1964–1992.

In the second Scheme of Control, despite high inflation rates throughout the period, the real rates of return on equity enjoyed by the two companies increased. The changes in the rates of return can partly explain why the first Scheme had a greater impact on reducing electricity prices than did the second Scheme. But we still have to evaluate whether these actual rates of return earned by the two companies cover their capital costs.

The main problem associated with the CE method is that different companies may have different accounting methods, particularly in measuring depreciation. This is illustrated vividly in the case of HEC. Following the 1988 review of the Scheme of Control, the useful lives of certain fixed assets of the company were revised upwards. This revision may have affected HEC's book rates of return after 1988. Moreover, the accounting policies applied to the two electricity companies are slightly different,[4] even though they are both subject to the Scheme of Control. Taking these problems into account, we find that

---

4. Compare *The Schemes of Control* (Hong Kong Government 1982b), p. 13 with p. 83.

the CE method is not a good method of measuring the costs of capital of the two electricity companies.

(2) The Dividend Growth Model (DGM)

In the 1980s, the dividend growth model (DGM) or the discounted cash flows method replaced the CE method and became the most widely used alternative of measuring the cost of capital for regulated firms in the United States. There are a few assumptions behind the method:

    (a) future dividends are expected to grow at a constant rate perpetually;

    (b) future dividends can be discounted at a constant cost of equity capital;

    (c) future dividends remain a constant proportion of earnings over time;

    (d) the firm is an all-equity-financed firm, or it has a constant level of leverage (or a constant debt-equity ratio).

The DGM relies on the equivalence of the market price of a stock, P_o, with the present value of the dividends (or cash flows) expected from the stock. The discount rate in finding the present value is considered to be the cost of equity capital. The present value (PV) of a stream of dividends (or cash flows) is often written as:

$$PV = D_1/(1+r) + D_2/(1+r)^2 + D_3/(1+r)^3 + \dots$$

$$PV = \sum [D_t/(1+r)^t],$$

where D_t is the expected dividend in year t, r is the discount rate or the cost of equity capital. If we assume that D_1 grows at a constant rate of g, then the present value of a stream of dividends (or cash flows) is:

$$PV = D_1/(1+r) + D_1(1+g)/(1+r)^2 + D_1(1+g)^2/(1+r)^3 + \dots$$

By substitutions, we obtain:

$$PV = D_1/(1+r) \times (1+r)/(r - g)$$
$$= D_1/(r - g).$$

Under competition, the price of an asset (P_0) is equal to the present value of its future cash flows. Hence we have:

$$P_0 = D_1/(r - g),$$

which says that the price of a stock at time 0 is the dividend expected at the end of the first-year, divided by the cost of equity capital minus the steady future growth rate of dividends. From the above equation, we obtain:

$$r = (D_1/P_0) + g.$$

To use the DGM to measure the costs of equity capital for the power companies we use five year historical data on dividends to estimate the expected dividends (D_1) and the growth rates (g). The data are shown in Table 6.3.

The discount rates (see Table 6.3) which measure the costs of equity capital are based on the geometric annual growth rates, over the period 1987–1992. Results are listed below:

CLP: $(1.04 \times 1.199/33.0) + 0.199 = 23.7\%$
HEC: $(0.82 \times 1.133/15.6) + 0.133 = 19.3\%$
HKG: $(0.34 \times 1.212/15.7) + 0.212 = 23.8\%$

HEC has a tradition of a higher dividend pay-out ratio than CLP, but its growth potential is constrained by the smaller territory it serves. From the above figures, CLP's cost of equity capital is much higher than that of HEC. Once again, we find that HKG has a higher discount rate than the other two regulated utilities.

Another approach to estimating the growth rate (g) of a company's stock is to find the "sustainable growth rate", which is the sum of the return on equity (ROE) and the plough-back ratio or retention ratio (b). This approach seeks to model the relationship between the "ploughing-back" of shareholders' earnings into the business and the resulting increase in dividends in the future. By using this approach, we can find the cost of equity capital (r) as follows:

$$r = (D_1/P_0) + g$$
$$= (D_1/P_0) + ROE \times b.$$

Table 6.3 Dividend and Dividend per Share*

Year	CLP Dividend (in HK$m)	CLP Dividend per share (in HK$)	HEC** Dividend (in HK$m)	HEC** Dividend per share (in HK$)	HKG Dividend (in HK$m)	HKG Dividend per share (in HK$)
1987	691	0.42	848	0.44	168	0.13
1988	829	0.50	983	0.49	204	0.16
1989	995	0.60	1,102	0.54	245	0.19
1990	1,194	0.72	1,232	0.61	294	0.23
1991	1,443	0.87	1,414	0.70	360	0.27
1992	1,725	1.04	1,657	0.82	445	0.34
Annual growth	20.1%	19.9%	14.3%	13.3%	21.5%	21.2%

Notes: * Figures are adjusted for new shares issued.
          ** Figures before Group reorganization are not shown.
Source: Annual reports of CLP, HEC, and HKG, 1987–1992.

If it is assumed that the company is always expected to earn an actual return on equity equal to its cost of capital, i.e. ROE = r, then we can simplify the above equation as follows:

$$r = (D_1/P_0) + r \times b$$
$$r(1 - b) = (D_1/P_0)$$
$$r = (D_1/P_0)/(1 - b),$$

where (D_1/P_0) is the current dividend yield of a company and (1 – b) is its pay-out ratio. The use of plough-back ratio (or pay-out ratio) may underestimate the growth rate of a company because it assumes a constant debt-equity ratio and ignores the fact that the two electricity companies can increase debts and development funds to finance expansion. If the two electricity companies issue debts to expand production capacity, their earnings and dividends will increase. But their costs of equity capital may also change. Furthermore, a company's dividend policy may change over time. In other words, the pay-out ratio (1 – b) is not a constant. Therefore, using historical data to estimate growth rate may not reflect a company's growth potential or its underlying cost of capital.

To conclude, the fundamental problem of the DGM is that it does not explicitly account for risk. The method assumes a constant level of leverage and future dividends are known with certainty. However, changes in a company's capital structure and dividend policy will affect the risk of holding the company's stock. This will, in turn, affect the cost of equity capital. The subsequent effects due to a change in leverage cannot be investigated by the DGM. The two electricity companies relied heavily on debt financing in the 1980s, and their capital structures changed substantially over time. In this respect, we have some reservations about the use of the DGM method to estimate the cost of equity capital. In the 1980s, there was a tendency for regulators in the United States and the United Kingdom to use the capital asset pricing model (CAPM) to estimate capital cost.

6.3 Capital Asset Pricing Model (CAPM)

The capital asset pricing model (CAPM) proposes that the current risk-return line is given by:

$$E(r_e) = r_f + \beta[E(r_m) - r_f],$$

where $E(r_e)$ = the expected rate of return for the regulated company's stock, r_f = the current risk-free rate of return, β = the stock's beta, $E(r_m)$ = the expected rate of return for the market, and $[E(r_m) - r_f]$ = risk premium. If the market is efficient, the cost of equity capital will be equal to the expected rate of return.

Therefore, if we use the CAPM to estimate a firm's cost of equity capital (or the required rate of return), we have to estimate a firm's beta, the risk-free rate of return, and the market risk premium (the difference between $E(r_m)$ and r_f).

(1) The Beta Value (β)

The return on a share of common stock comes from: capital gain ($P_t - P_{t-1}$) and dividends, (D_t). The one-period rate of return of a stock, r_t, is equal to the return divided by the beginning-of-period price:

$$r_t = (P_t - P_{t-1})/P_{t-1} + D_t/P_{t-1}$$
$$= (P_t + D_t)/P_{t-1} - 1.$$

To estimate the beta values of the regulated companies, we apply the following regression which assumes the CAPM or the market model is true:

$$r_t = a + \beta\, r_{mt} + \in,$$

where r_{mt} is the actual rate of return from the market portfolio and $\in$ is a random-error term. The above equation assumes that the return on an asset r_t is a linear function of the market portfolio proxy.

The beta coefficients of the two electricity companies are estimated by using ordinary least-squares (OLS) regression of the realized returns of the stocks on the market returns in each period, based on the daily and monthly share prices (closing prices). We have two sets of share price data in hand — one is daily share prices from January 1980 to December 1990 for CLP and HEC, while the other one is monthly share prices from January 1977 to December 1992. Results from both sets of data are reported. In Hong Kong, the Hang Seng Index (HSI) is often used as the market portfolio proxy. The Hang Seng Index is an arithmetic index of price relatives which covers 33 larger companies (called "blue chips") in Hong Kong. We have also adopted Dimson's (1979) approach which is designed to tackle the non-trading problem. Dimson's approach involves running a regression similar to the above market model but where both leading and lagging terms in the market return are included. The regression equation used in Dimson's approach is similar but includes a number of leading and lagging terms:

$$r_t = \alpha + \sum_{i=-K}^{+K} \beta_i\, r_{mt+i} + \in,$$

The leading and lagging terms capture the correlation between the share's return and the market's return which is lost because of non-synchronous trading between the share and the market portfolio. Daily or weekly data is more likely to suffer from this non-trading problem as compared with monthly data. In our estimation, we also employ Dimson's approach by using one leading term and one lagging term. The regression equation is:

$r_t = \alpha + \beta_{t-1}r_{mt-1} + \beta_t r_{mt} + \beta_{t+1}r_{mt+1} + \epsilon,$

Because of the lack of cross-sectional information about the beta values and standard errors of all individual shares in the market, we cannot make a Bayesian adjustment to our estimates of beta values. We estimate the beta values of six public utilities (all but one have been under Schemes of Control, see p. 115) in Hong Kong and our results are shown in Table 6.4.

From our estimations based on monthly data, we find the beta values of these six companies are as follows:

Company	Beta Value
CLP	0.93
HEC	0.79
HKG	0.96
HKT	0.76
KMB	0.71
CMB	0.83

Our results are quite consistent with an earlier study conducted by Pak (1983). Pak estimated the average beta values for CLP and HKT, using monthly returns for the period from August 1969 to December 1982. His results suggest that the average beta value for CLP is 0.94 and that for HKT is 0.83. HKT has a lower beta value compared to CLP. The unregulated utility, HKG, has the highest beta value. This result is not unexpected as the Scheme of Control (with the formation of development funds) reduces profit fluctuations of the regulated firms.

Our results show that both electricity companies have beta values below one. This is not unexpected as their returns are regulated by the Government. However, the beta values estimated from monthly data are quite different from those estimated from daily data. When monthly data are used, CLP has a higher beta (0.93) than HEC (0.79 or 0.73), but when daily data are used, their beta values are quite similar. In the United Kingdom, the beta values of some regulated utilities drop significantly when the figures of the 1987 stock market crash are excluded. However, we do not observe such a situation in

Table 6.4 Summary of Equity Beta Calculations

(A) Beta Estimates from Monthly and Daily Data

Company	Period	Monthly Beta	R^2	Daily Beta	R^2
CLP	1977–1992	0.93 (0.04)	0.75	N.A.	
	1980–1990	0.93 (0.05)	0.76	0.85 (0.02)	0.37
HEC	1977–1992	0.79 (0.04)	0.69	N.A.	
	1980–1992	0.73 (0.04)	0.68	0.86 (0.01)	0.60
HKG	1977–1992	0.96 (0.05)	0.62	N.A.	
HKT	1977–1992	0.76 (0.05)	0.51	N.A.	
KMB	1977–1992	0.71 (0.08)	0.32	N.A.	
CMB	1977–1992	0.83 (0.09)	0.29	N.A.	

(B) Aggregate Coefficient (Dimson) Betas: Monthly Data (1977–1992)

Company		r_{mt-1}	r_{mt}	r_{mt+1}	Aggregate Beta	R^2
CLP	Coeff	−0.06	0.94	−0.03	0.85	0.76
	S.E.	(0.04)	(0.04)	(0.04)		
HEC	Coeff	−0.01	0.79	−0.08	0.70	0.70
	S.E.	(0.04)	(0.04)	(0.04)		
HKG	Coeff	−0.01	0.96	−0.07	0.88	0.63
	S.E.	(0.06)	(0.06)	(0.06)		
HKT	Coeff	0.02	0.77	−0.15	0.77	0.54
	S.E.	(0.05)	(0.05)	(0.05)		
KMB	Coeff	0.20	0.71	−0.10	0.80	0.35
	S.E.	(0.8)*	(0.07)	(0.07)		
CMB	Coeff	0.25	0.82	0.06	1.13	0.32
	S.E.	(0.09)*	(0.09)	(0.09)		

Notes: Standard errors in parentheses.
N.A. = data are not available.
* Significant at the 5% level.

our study. When the monthly data of the 1987 market crash (i.e. October 1987) are excluded, the beta values of CLP and HEC do not change significantly.

Returning to Dimson's approach, we find that the non-trading problem is not serious in estimating the beta values of CLP and HEC, since the stocks of the two companies are frequently traded in the market. All the leading and lagging terms are insignificant at the 5% level. However, there is evidence of a non-trading problem for the two bus companies (KMB and CMB), particularly for the smaller of the two, CMB. Transactions of the shares of the two companies in the market are less frequent, as compared with the shares of other larger regulated utilities. Adding the leading and lagging terms in our regressions raise the R-square and the beta coefficient. Furthermore, the lagging terms for both companies are significant at the 5% level. In view of these findings, we should be cautious in estimating the beta values of KMB and CMB.

To consider the stability of beta over time, we use daily data to estimate the two electricity companies' beta values each year. For the monthly data, we estimate the betas of the two stocks for each five year period (60 months). We start with the period from January 1981 to December 1985 and end with the period from January 1986 to December 1990.[5] In covering a ten year period, we can readily compare the beta for the first five years with that for the last five years in the 1980s. Figure 6.1 shows the beta values (based on monthly data for every five years) of the two electricity companies over time.

The beta values obtained from daily data fluctuate greatly, ranging from 0.61 to 1.02 for CLP and from 0.59 to 1.14 for HEC. But the beta values obtained from monthly data are quite stable. The beta values of CLP are more stable than those of HEC over the period. The beta of CLP lies between 0.87 and 0.99, and it stays around 0.93 most of the time. In the early period, the beta value of CLP decreases steadily until it reaches the lowest value in mid-1987. After that, the value of beta increases and remains relatively stable. Hence, a figure of 0.93 (based on monthly data) seems to be a good estimate of CLP's beta value.

---

5. We do not use data after 1990 so as to avoid the problems arising from the two companies' recent involvement in property development.

Figure 6.1   Beta Values of CLP and HEC

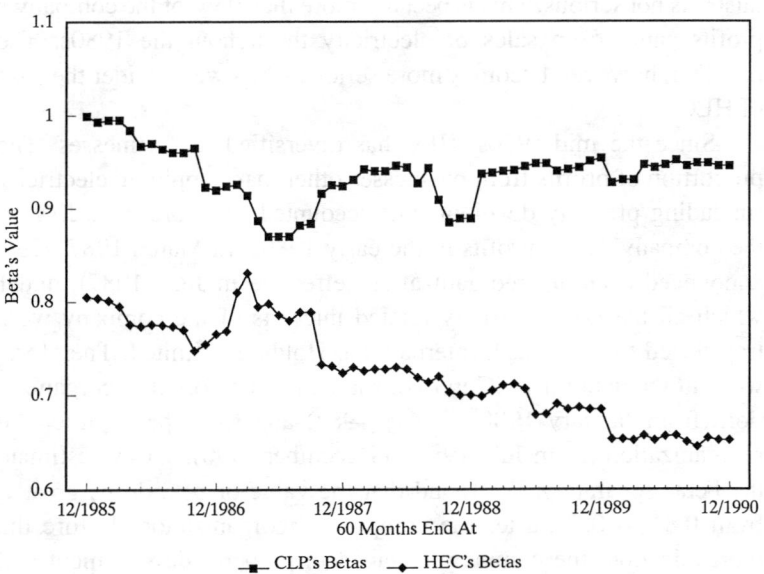

On the other hand, it is more difficult to estimate HEC's beta value. The beta value of the company changes from 0.73 to 0.79 (see Table 6.4) when data based on a longer period are used. From Figure 6.1, we can see that the beta value of HEC peaked at 0.83 in March 1987, it decreased steadily and reached a minimum of 0.65 (which is also the beta value for the last five years). The R-square of the regression, which indicates the proportion of systematic (non-diversifiable) risk, also decreased steadily, from 0.80 to 0.58. One plausible reason for the changes in HEC's beta value is the Group's reorganization in 1987.

As mentioned before, both electricity companies have engaged in businesses other than supplying electricity. Therefore, we should be careful in using the beta values of these two companies, since our purpose is to measure the cost of capital invested in the electricity industry only, rather than the cost of capital invested in all businesses. For CLP, the problem of distinguishing the beta value of the company from the beta value of an investment project in the electricity industry is not serious. This is because more than 95% of the company's profits came from sales of electricity throughout the 1980s. The problem, however, becomes more serious when we consider the case of HEC.

Since the mid-1970s, HEC has diversified its businesses. The proportion of profits from businesses other than supplying electricity (including property development) accounted for more than 20% of the company's total profits in the early 1980s. In March 1987, HEC announced a Group reorganization (effective in June 1987), under which all the non-electricity related interests of the company were transferred to Cavendish International Holdings Limited. Therefore, we split the data for HEC in two: share prices before the reorganization (from January 1980 to May 1987) and share prices after the reorganization (from July 1987 to December 1990), and we estimate the betas separately. We found that the value of beta drops greatly, from 0.81 to 0.59, after the company's reorganization. Before the reorganization, the company engaged in property development and the profit earned was more unstable. After the reorganization, the firm has concentrated on electricity supply which provides a more stable income. As a result, the market risk of the company may have decreased. If we take the figure after the Group's reorganization as our estimate of HEC's beta value, we arrive at a relatively low value of 0.59.

(2) Risk-Free Rate (r_f)

In Hong Kong, the monetary authority only started issuing bonds (called Exchange Fund Bills) in early 1990. To date, we do not have sufficient information about the market interest rates on these bonds to measure the risk-free rate. As a result, we have to choose another proxy to measure the risk-free rate.

Some analysts (like Pak in 1983) have previously used time deposit rates as proxies for the risk-free rates. More recently, in a report called *Review on Government Utilities* (Hong Kong Government, Finance Branch 1994), the Government suggested the yield from seven-year Mass Transit Railway (MTR) bonds as the risk-free rate. This implies an 8.22% risk-free rate. However, we do not think that these are good proxies. From historical data, the real interest rates on time deposits (less than $500,000) are often found to be negative (see Table 6.5). The Interest Rate Rules in Hong Kong tended to protect the licensed banks at the expense of small depositors. The use of the yield from MTR bonds is also not appropriate due to its relatively short existence.

In Hong Kong, many large companies (including those under the Schemes of Control) are family-owned. Members from the same family usually hold more than 30 percent of the shares of the company. Such a huge amount of capital can of course obtain better yields from other investment opportunities than from investing at the time deposit rates (which are negative in real terms). One alternative is to loan out the money in the inter-bank money market. The arithmetic mean of inter-bank one month or three month interest rate is about 9% for the period 1981–1992 (see Table 6.5). Another investment alternative for these large companies under the Schemes of Control is to act like licensed banks and to loan out the capital fund to earn the prime rate (or the best lending rate). The prime rate is the lending rate charged by commercial banks on loans made to their best lenders (the customers with the lowest default risks). This reflects the cost of debt capital which is more or less risk-free. If we use the prime rate as a proxy for the risk-free rate, the arithmetic mean of the annual nominal prime rate (based on monthly data) for the period 1964–1992 is also

Table 6.5   Interest Rates in Hong Kong

Period	Prime rate	Deposit rate			Inter-bank rate		Inflation rate
		1-month	3-month	12-month	1-month	3-month	
1964–1992	8.9%	5.6%	6.0%	7.0%	N.A.	N.A.	7.6%
1977–1992	10.0%	5.3%	6.3%	7.3%	N.A.	N.A.	9.0%
1981–1992	10.3%	4.6%	6.7%	7.3%	9.4%	8.6%	8.7%

Sources: Hong Kong Government, Census and Statistics Department 1967; 1970–1993; 1970–1995.

about 9% (see Table 6.5). Hence, a risk-free rate of 9% can serve as a good proxy in our cost of capital estimation.[6]

(3) Risk Premium $(E(r_m) - r_f)$

The CAPM is a forward looking model which relates the expected return on an asset to the expected return on the market as a whole over some future period. The expected return on the market, however, is not observable and must be estimated. The most common method used to estimate the expected market risk premium is based on histori-cal data. If the degree of risk aversion of market participants and the level of uncertainty are stable over time, the long-run average realized rate of return provides an estimate of the *ex-ante* risk premium.

The base period of the Hang Seng Index is 31 July 1964. Our estimate of the risk premium is based on the historical data of the Index from 1964 to 1992. The market risk premium can be calculated on the basis of an arithmetic mean or geometric mean of past equity returns. There is a strong theoretical case, however, for using the arithmetic rather than the geometric mean. The geometric mean of past returns is not the same as the expected future return unless there is complete certainty. It is argued that, unless the regulator adopts a system of *ex-post* regulation to guarantee returns, regulated firms do not operate under complete certainty and so the arithmetic mean should be used.[7] Table 6.6 shows our estimates of the risk premium on equities (based on the arithmetic means) in Hong Kong. The arith-metic mean of annual nominal returns on equities over different periods is estimated by using both monthly and annual data.

Since our estimates of the beta values are based on monthly data, we are inclined to accept the risk premium figure based on the

---

6. Data since the issue of government bonds in 1990 suggest that interest rates on three month Exchange Fund Bills are between inter-bank three month interest rates and the prime rate, about 0.5% above the inter-bank rate.
7. For a detailed discussion on arithmetic and geometric means, please refer to Water Services Association (UK) and Water Companies Association 1991, Vol. 3, Appendix 2.

Table 6.6 Estimates of the Risk Premium on Equities

(A) Monthly Data			
Period	Equity return	Prime rate	Risk premium
1964–1992	20.4%	9.0%	11.4%
1977–1992	20.8%	10.0%	10.8%
1981–1992	16.1%	10.3%	5.8%
(B) Annual Data			
Period	Equity return	Prime rate	Risk premium
1964–1992	24.1%	9.0%	15.1%
1977–1992	21.2%	10.0%	11.2%
1981–1992	15.1%	10.3%	4.8%

monthly return on equities, rather than that based on the annual return on equities. Hence, a risk premium of 11%, based on a longer period of average realized rates of return (1964–1992) is used in our analysis.

(4) Expected Rates of Return ($E(r_e)$)

Using our estimates of beta values, the risk-free rate (9%), and the market risk premium (11%), we work out the expected rates of return on equity capital of the two electricity companies in Hong Kong. Our results are shown below:

CLP: $9.0\% + 0.93(11\%) = 19.2\%$
HEC: $9.0\% + 0.81(11\%) = 17.9\%$ (before reorganization)
         $9.0\% + 0.59(11\%) = 15.5\%$ (after reorganization)
HKG: $9.0\% + 0.96(11\%) = 19.6\%$
HKT: $9.0\% + 0.76(11\%) = 17.4\%$
KMB: $9.0\% + 0.71(11\%) = 16.8\%$
CMB: $9.0\% + 0.83(11\%) = 18.1\%$

If we use the yield from seven year Mass Transit Railway (MTR) bonds (or other deposit rates) as the risk-free rate, then the expected rates of return on equity capital would be lower. Nevertheless, our results are again consistent with the results obtained from other methods. Because of its higher market risk, HKG's stock has a higher expected (or required) rate of return. It should be reiterated that by debt financing, the two electricity companies can earn returns on equity exceeding the permitted rate of 15%. Even though the permitted rate on equity may be lower than the expected rate, CLP and HEC can actually earn returns higher than their costs of capital. Since the permitted return on equity for the two electricity companies under the second Scheme of Control (from 1979 to 1993) is 15%, which is lower than the required rate of return, we would expect the two companies to have less incentive to expand by equity-financing. They would rely more on debt financing as the permitted return (13%) is higher than the cost of debt capital (about 8%). This implies that even though the permitted rate of return on equity is less than the required rate, the two regulated companies could still earn an actual rate of return on equity higher than the cost of equity capital by relying on debt financing.

We may compare the above expected rates of return with the actual rates of return on equity earned by these companies. As seen from Table 6.1 and Table 6.2, these three power companies earned returns more than the rates justified by their systematic risks during the period from 1977 to 1992.

6.4 Effects of Capital Structure on Capital Cost

For a leveraged firm, the beta value measures the business as well as the financial risk faced by the shareholders of the firm. Literature in finance theory argues that having a higher debt-equity ratio will increase a firm's financial risk and beta value. Given the high and unstable debt-equity ratios (D/E) of the three power companies (see Table 6.7), we may doubt the stability of their betas over time. It should also be noted that under the existing Scheme of Control, the development funds (T) are treated as liabilities of the regulated utilities. Hence, if the development funds are included in the calculation, the debt plus development fund-equity ratios ((D+T)/E) of the two electricity companies would then be even higher (see Table 6.7). Because CLP joined the Scheme earlier than HEC, the relative size of

Table 6.7 Debt-Equity Ratios (in HK$ million)

(A) When development funds (T) are not included

Year	CLP* Debt	CLP* Equity	CLP* D/E	HEC** Debt	HEC** Equity	HEC** D/E	HKG Debt	HKG Equity	HKG D/E
1978	46	1,714	2.7%	221	1,455	15.2%	32	148	21.6%
1979	678	2,214	30.6%	338	1,584	21.3%	48	159	30.2%
1980	2,153	2,531	85.1%	633	3,380	18.7%	40	265	15.1%
1981	4,114	3,575	115.1%	1,172	3,673	31.9%	135	447	30.2%
1982	5,355	4,393	121.9%	1,128	4,258	26.5%	179	490	36.5%
1983	8,267	5,224	158.3%	965	4,661	20.7%	212	554	38.3%
1984	8,764	6,028	145.4%	995	4,758	20.9%	260	644	40.4%
1985	11,001	6,545	168.1%	2,477	5,297	46.8%	290	1,094	26.5%
1986	10,434	8,562	121.9%	2,372	7,083	33.5%	377	1,277	29.5%
1987	9,935	10,026	99.1%	1,930	6,055	31.9%	436	1,428	30.5%
1988	9,086	11,460	79.3%	2,495	6,616	37.7%	442	1,648	26.8%
1989	8,197	12,741	64.3%	3,504	7,225	48.5%	682	1,938	35.2%
1990	8,623	14,068	61.3%	3,570	7,921	45.1%	1,124	2,229	50.4%
1991	9,002	15,482	58.1%	4,909	8,849	55.5%	1,469	2,709	54.2%
1992	9,173	16,906	54.3%	5,422	10,242	52.9%	1,316	3,203	41.1%

(B) When development funds (T) are included

Year	CLP* Dev Fund	CLP* T/E	CLP* (D+T)/E	HEC Dev Fund	HEC T/E	HEC (D+T)/E
1978	197	11.1%	13.8%	0	0%	15.2%
1979	170	7.7%	38.3%	0	0%	21.3%
1980	164	6.5%	91.5%	4	0%†	18.8%
1981	178	5.0%	120.0%	3	0%†	32.0%
1982	228	5.2%	127.1%	5	0%†	26.6%
1983	323	6.2%	164.4%	155	3.3%	24.0%
1984	449	7.4%	152.8%	258	5.4%	26.3%
1985	548	8.4%	176.5%	301	5.7%	52.4%
1986	955	11.2%	133.0%	335	4.7%	38.2%
1987	1,458	14.5%	113.6%	445	7.3%	39.2%
1988	1,958	17.1%	95.5%	425	6.4%	44.1%
1989	2,246	17.6%	82.0%	560	7.8%	56.2%
1990	2,710	19.3%	80.6%	426	5.4%	50.4%
1991	2,849	18.4%	76.5%	473	5.3%	60.8%
1992	3,222	19.1%	73.3%	397	3.9%	56.8%

Notes: * Figures include CLP's associated generating companies.
** Debt figures for HEC are long-term liabilities; the company was reorganized in 1987 and its debt and equity were restructured.
† Less than 0.1%.

Sources: Annual reports of CLP, HEC and HKG, 1978–1992.

the former's development fund is much larger than the latter's. By the early 1980s, CLP had already accumulated a sizable development fund which was used to a large extent to finance CLP's expansion. On the other hand, as the expansion of HEC is limited by its smaller service area, the use of the development fund or debt to finance expansion is also limited. As seen from Table 6.7, for the period 1988–1992, the development fund-equity ratio (T/E) of CLP is 18%, as compared to 5% for HEC.

Finance theories have argued that a higher debt-equity ratio (D/E) will raise the equity beta of a firm, yet leave the firm's overall cost of capital (r) unchanged. However, as long as the development fund is sufficient to compensate any shortfalls in realized profits, it is guaranteed that the regulated firm will earn the permitted rate of return. Fluctuations in realized profit will not increase the risk borne by the shareholders. A direct testable implication then follows: a higher debt-equity ratio will increase the rate of return on equity, but it will not raise the financial risk or beta of a regulated company. Under the Scheme of Control, with a sufficient development fund a higher debt-equity ratio raises the rate of return on equity, but it leaves the financial risk unchanged.

Did the reliance on debt financing raise the beta values of the two electricity companies? In Table 6.8, we show the debt-equity ratios, development fund-equity ratios, and beta values (based on monthly data) of the two electricity companies for each five year period. From Table 6.8, we can see the debt-equity ratio of CLP increases from 0.71 to 1.43 and then decreases to 0.63, but its beta value only ranges from 0.88 to 0.97. Empirical data seem to support the notion that with the existence of a development fund, a higher debt-equity ratio does not imply higher financial risk. Higher debt-equity ratios of the two electricity companies were accompanied by higher rates of return on equity, but the beta values of the two companies did not increase when more debts were incurred. On the contrary, when more debts in the form of development fund were issued, the beta values were lower. The value of beta for CLP was relatively stable in the 1980s even though the debt-equity ratio of the company varied greatly over time. For HEC, despite the fact that its debt-equity ratio increased gradually

Table 6.8 Debts and Beta Values

Period	CLP D/E	CLP T/E	CLP Beta	HEC D/E	HEC T/E	HEC Beta
1978–82	0.71	0.07	0.97	0.23	0	0.94
1979–83	1.02	0.06	0.97	0.24	0.01	0.87
1980–84	1.25	0.06	0.94	0.24	0.02	0.76
1981–85	1.42	0.06	0.96	0.29	0.03	0.80
1982–86	1.43	0.08	0.96	0.30	0.04	0.77
1983–87	1.38	0.10	0.88	0.31	0.05	0.72
1984–88	1.22	0.12	0.91	0.34	0.06	0.70
1985–89	1.06	0.14	0.94	0.40	0.06	0.69
1986–90	0.85	0.16	0.95	0.39	0.06	0.65
1987–91	0.72	0.17	0.93	0.44	0.06	0.63
1988–92	0.63	0.18	0.92	0.48	0.06	0.62

over time, its beta value dropped significantly only after the Group's reorganization in 1987.

6.5 Comparisons

(1) Comparison with Other Utilities in Hong Kong

In Hong Kong, seven companies have been subject to the Scheme of Control. Apart from the two electricity companies, two franchised bus companies, one local telephone company, and two companies providing airport services (air cargo and air terminal services) have also been under the Scheme of Control. Table 6.9 shows the main terms in their respective Schemes of Control.

Since the two companies providing airport services are not separately listed on the stock market, they are not included in our study. The Scheme of Control was first proposed by CLP in 1964. Later, when the Hong Kong Government renewed the franchises with the two bus companies and the telephone company in 1975, profit control schemes were added. The permitted returns are based on average net assets except for the telephone company (its permitted return is based on equity). We compare the required (or expected) rates of return (on equity) and permitted rates of return under the Scheme of Control.

	Required rate on equity	Permitted rate	
		on debt	on equity
CLP	19.2%	13.5%	15%
HEC	17.9%	13.5%	15%
	(before reorganization)		
	15.5%		
	(after reorganization)		
HKT	17.4%	0%	16%
KMB	16.8%	16.0%	16%
CMB	18.1%	15.0%	15%

The above figures suggest that the required rates of return on equity (costs of equity capital), for all these regulated utilities, are higher than the permitted rates. However, it should be noted that they still enjoy an actual rate of return on equity (see Table 6.1 and Table 6.2) higher than both the required and the permitted rate on equity by debt financing. This is made possible by arbitrage as the permitted rate on debt is higher than the cost of debt capital.

As mentioned earlier, every dollar used in acquiring fixed assets for generating electricity, if financed by debt or the development fund, enables the electricity companies to enjoy 13.5 cents of permitted return. The maximum deduction is just 8 cents from the permitted return, which goes into the rate reduction reserve. This explains why the two electricity utilities can earn a rate of return on equity exceeding 20%, even though the permitted return on equity capital is restricted to 15%. As the permitted rate of return on equity is less than the required rate, the two companies prefer debt financing to equity financing. This also explains why the equity values of the two companies have grown more slowly than their asset values.

We have observed a similar situation in KMB, the largest franchised bus company in Hong Kong. The company has been relying more and more on debt to finance expansion. For CMB, its expansion has been limited by the smaller service area and the completion of the Mass Transit Railway (Hong Kong Island extension). In 1993, some of CMB's routes were transferred by the Transport

Table 6.9 Regulated Companies under the Scheme of Control

Company	Effectiver period	Permitted return
China Light and Power Company Ltd. (CLP)	10/1963–9/1978	13.5% of average net fixed assets
	10/1978–9/1993	13.5% of average net fixed assets plus 1.5% for shareholders' investment
	10/1993–9/2008	Same as above
Hongkong Electric Company Ltd. (HEC)	1/1979–12/1993	13.5% of average net fixed assets plus 1.5% for shareholders' investment
	1/1994–12/2008	Same as above
Hong Kong Telephone Company Ltd. (HKT)	1/1976–6/1995	16% of shareholders' funds (development fund exhausted in 1991, replaced by price-cap regulation for the period 7/1992–6/1995)
Kowloon Motor Bus Company Ltd. (KMB)	9/1975–8/1987	16% of average net fixed assets
	9/1987–8/1997 (renewed for every two years)	Same as above
China Motor Bus Company Ltd. (CMB)	9/1975–8/1987	15% of average net fixed assets
	9/1987–8/1993 (renewed for every two years)	Same as above
Hong Kong Air Cargo Services Ltd.	5/1/1975–27/1/1997	12.5% of gross value of assets
Hong Kong Air Terminal Services Ltd.	7/1979–6/1985	18% of average net fixed assets
	7/1985–12/1996	Same as above

Sources: Hong Kong Government 1982b, p. 2.
           Ming Pao, 2 December 1992.

Department to another operator, Citybus. The company's bus fleet was then contracted. As a result, expansion through debt financing has been further restrained. Furthermore, since 1987, the Government renewed the Scheme of Control with the company on a short-term basis (two years), thus causing difficulty in arranging long-term loans. In fact, CMB has not issued any long-term debt since 1989.[8] A required rate of return higher than the permitted rate implies that the revenue of the company cannot cover its cost. If this is the case, CMB will not replace capital in the long run. This helps explain why the company has continued to use second-hand buses and why its services have been deteriorating over time.

Lastly, we would like to discuss briefly the case of HKT. HKT merged with Hong Kong Telecommunications International (HKTI) in 1987 to form Hong Kong Telecommunications. In January 1988, as part of the merger arrangement, Hong Kong Telecommunications replaced the listing position of HKT in the Hong Kong Stock Exchange. After the merger, Hong Kong Telecommunications was accused of using some of its surplus from international calls to subsidize the local telephone company (Mueller 1991). Instead of raising local telephone tariffs, HKT used the development fund and the subsidy to compensate any shortfalls in the permitted return. The development fund was depleted in 1991 and HKT negotiated with the Government to shift from the Scheme of Control to the existing price-cap regulation. Hence, if Hong Kong Telecommunications has been adopting a pricing policy of cross-subsidization, then it is not important whether HKT (providing local telephone service) was able to earn a permitted rate of return covering the cost of capital.

(2) Comparison with Utilities in the United Kingdom and the United States

As the Scheme of Control in Hong Kong is different from regulations in the United States and the United Kingdom, it might be helpful to make some crude comparisons in the beta values of public utilities in these three places. Table 6.10 shows the beta values (without Bayesian adjustment) of public utilities in the United Kingdom and

---

8. From CMB's annual reports, there is no interest charge on long-term financing since 1989. Even for years before 1989, interest charges are very small, which suggests that the comnpany did not rely heavily on debt-financing.

Table 6.10 Beta Values of U.K. and U.S. Utilities

	Equity Beta	Asset Beta
U.K.*		
British Telecom	0.77	0.66
	(0.70)	(0.55)
British Gas	0.79	0.63
	(0.68)	(0.51)
British Airport Authority	0.77	0.54
	(0.61)	(0.55)
Water Utilities	0.57	0.47
U.S.		
Public Utilities	0.33*	0.30**
U.S. Electric Utilities#		
— unregulated	0.70	
— weakly regulated	0.64	
— strongly regulated	0.58	
Water Companies[t]	0.32	

Sources: * Water Services Association (UK) and Water Companies Association 1991, p. 117. Figures in brackets are from Beesley 1992, pp. 92–93.
** Litzenberger *et al.* 1980, p. 380.
# Norton 1985, p. 677.
[t] Beesley 1992, pp. 92–93.

the United States. In general, we find that regulated utilities in the United Kingdom have higher beta values than their counterparts in the United States. These results are not unexpected, since the rate-of-return regulation in the United States lowers the risk and the cost of capital. In the United Kingdom, however, the wider use of the price-cap regulation in the 1980s, which allows the prospect of wider variation in realized rates of return, raises the risk and the beta value of a regulated utility.

The difference in beta values between utilities in these two countries suggests that one cannot ignore the effect of the regulatory system on the cost of capital. A change in the regulatory system would also affect the systematic risk faced by the regulated utility. As U.S. regulation is providing less of an insurance policy for poor management practices (there are now a number of experiments in the use of incentive-based, price-cap regulation), there has been a long-term trend for betas across the utility sector to rise (Water Services Association (UK) and Water Companies Association 1991, p. 64). As compared with the beta values of U.K. and U.S. utilities, firms under the Schemes of Control in Hong Kong have higher beta values. This can be partly explained by the fact that some of these regulated utilities in Hong Kong are involved in other more risky non-regulated businesses which raises the beta values of the stocks. The main reason for higher beta values, however, is due to the regulatory system itself. Since the Scheme of Control regulates the nominal returns, rather than the real returns, the real returns of regulated utilities are greatly affected by inflation. As the inflation rate in Hong Kong rises and varies over time, the real returns earned by these regulated utilities will also fluctuate.

CHAPTER 7

Conclusion and Recommendations

7.1 Regulatory Behaviour under the Scheme of Control

For historical and economic reasons, the two electricity companies in Hong Kong have become regional monopolists. Each company supplies electricity to a particular area and there is no direct competition between the two companies. This situation allowed the two companies to earn a real rate of return on equity more than 22% in the 1950s. This high real rate of return, coupled with rising surcharges on fuel, resulted in the Government's intervention. An Electricity Supply Company Commission was set up in 1959 to look into ways of controlling these two regional monopolists.

Instead of adopting the British-type of nationalization policy recommended by the Commission, the Government accepted CLP's rate-of-return control scheme, called the Scheme of Control. This control scheme has been applied for 30 years, and our findings suggest that it has affected electricity prices, organizational form and financial structure of the two regulated electricity companies.

During the first Scheme of Control (1964–1978) imposed on CLP, consumers enjoyed relatively lower tariffs and the company's real rate of return on equity was reduced to 9%. But CLP's subsidization policy in favour of industrial users continued. The Scheme also brought a partnership between CLP and Exxon, and the formation of their associated generating companies in the 1960s and 1970s.

After HEC formally joined the Scheme in 1979, the two electricity companies tried to increase their rates of return on equity by issuing debt. This was made possible as the permitted rate on debt was much higher than the cost of debt capital. The debt-equity ratio of CLP often exceeded one for a long period of time. Unlike the rate-of-return regulation in the United States, which measures debt cost, equity cost and then overall cost of capital, the Scheme of Control in Hong Kong fixes the overall cost of capital first. It was found that more debt did not raise the cost of equity capital if the development fund was sufficiently large. Through issuing debt, the two regulated electricity companies enjoyed high nominal rates of return on equity exceeding 20%, even though the permitted rates of return on equity and debt (both in nominal terms) were restricted to 15% and 13.5%, respectively. This means that consumers' benefits were not protected, and they had to pay higher prices in order to finance the companies' expansion. The Scheme of Control has substantially affected the financial structure of the two regulated utilities.[1]

The huge capital expenditures required to build coal-fired generators in the early 1980s led to drastic increases in electricity tariffs and an end of CLP's subsidization policy: industrial users no longer enjoyed cross-subsidy from other users. Because of diminishing political and economic influence, the protests of industrial users were to no avail. As HEC was a diversified company between 1976 and 1987, the Scheme of Control, which provides more or less guaranteed returns, might have encouraged cost-shifting and cross-subsidization within the company. Electricity consumers paid higher prices to subsidize the company's other activities. After the reorganization of the company in 1987, it was found that the company's cost of equity capital (measured by the beta) decreased. Here we can see the interaction between government regulation, price structure, organizational form and financial structure of a regulated firm. During this period, it seems that the Scheme of Control tended to protect the producers' interest.

---

1. Spiegel and Spulber (1994) have provided a different argument for a higher debt-equity ratio of regulated firms.

Our analysis suggests that the rate-of-return regulation based on the Scheme of Control, despite its early success, has failed to restrict the two electricity companies to earning a return on equity capital "which is reasonable in relation to the risks involved and the capital invested in and retained in the business". In addition, unless by coincidence, a fixed maximum interest rate (8%) charged on debts and the development fund cannot reflect the cost of debt capital correctly. The distortion is even more serious during periods of high nominal interest rates (e.g. in the early 1980s). Because the permitted rate of return on debt is higher than the cost of debt capital, regulated utilities can effectively get around the regulation on asset return by altering their capital structures and organizational forms. As long as the Government continues to rely on the Scheme of Control to prevent the utilities from earning excessive profits, some amendments should be made to improve the situation.

7.2 Recommendations

Empirical evidence has shown that the electricity industry can be regarded as a natural monopoly: average cost decreases when output increases. However, this does not necessarily imply that the service should be provided by one single firm or that competition cannot exist in the industry. Although some analysts have proposed the merging of the two companies or introducing other forms of regulation (such as the price-cap regulation), we hold the position that the two companies should remain separate entities and to make competition between them possible.

In addition, we support the original spirit of the Scheme of Control. Because of the nature of the electricity industry, such as demand uncertainty, asset specificity, and long planning horizon, a long-term contract protecting the producers' right to serve seems to be desirable. As producers' returns are protected to a certain extent, the Scheme of Control can introduce stability into the industry and facilitate debt financing. Financial institutions are then more willing to provide loans to the electricity companies and provide them at a lower cost.[2] Our studies also suggest that both consumers and producers can benefit from this arrangement. But given the recent changes in technology and operating environment in the industry, some tentative suggestions to improve the existing schemes are given below.

(1) Separating Electricity Supply from Other Businesses

It has been found that the beta value of a regulated firm was influenced by its organizational form. A diversified electricity firm has a higher beta value than a non-diversified one which concentrates on the regulated business (Robison *et al.* 1995). Since the major objective of any regulatory contract is to protect both producers' right to serve and consumers' right to be served, we should find ways to measure precisely the cost of capital employed in the regulated industry. In order for the regulator to apply finance theories to measure capital cost, the two electricity companies should not be allowed to engage in businesses other than electricity supply. They could form separate companies for other businesses. Such structural separation would also prevent cost-shifting and cross-subsidization within the firm.

(2) Improving the Scheme of Control

Some interest groups have long urged the Government to use shareholders' funds, instead of fixed assets, as the rate base on which to calculate the permitted return, for the purpose of avoiding over-expansion by the utilities. But their argument does not address the major problem of the Scheme. Our analysis has shown that the two electricity companies have little incentive to use shareholders' funds

---

2. In this regard, bus companies should not be protected by the Scheme of Control, since the industry is labour-intensive rather than capital-intensive. Sunk investment costs are relatively small and the assets of the companies can be easily resold in the resale market.

to finance capital expansion because the permitted rate of return on equity does not cover the equity cost, while the permitted rate on debt far exceeds the actual debt cost. If the permitted rate of return, either on equity capital or debt capital, is determined correctly to reflect their respective costs, then the regulated firm will be less inclined to increase the permitted return by changing its capital structure.

If fixed assets are maintained as the rate base, then the interest rate charged on debts and the development fund, instead of being fixed at a maximum of 8%, should be allowed to change in line with actual interest rate movements. Furthermore, the permitted return should be set in real terms, not in nominal terms. Instead of setting a fixed permitted rate on assets, the regulator should determine the equity cost, debt cost and inflation rate first, and then use the information to determine the overall cost of capital. The development fund could continue to serve as a return buffer for a regulated utility, as this reduces the risk faced by a regulated utility. Moreover, the development fund also provides some incentive for a regulated firm to lower cost so as to accumulate the fund.

To encourage efficient production, the rate-of-return regulation should be imposed together with the price-cap. We need simply to impose additional constraints on the existing price adjustment mechanism of the Scheme. Once the permitted rate has been determined, the regulator would allow a regulated utility to raise prices by a certain percentage below the change in the consumer price index. The price-cap so determined would then allow the utility to earn sufficient returns to cover its cost of capital. If the utility increases productivity at a rate faster than the X-factor (productivity gain), then it would be rewarded by earning more than the permitted returns.

Finally, we must recognize that it is impossible to choose a permitted rate of return which will reflect the cost of capital for such a long period of time as 15 years. Therefore, some interim reviews (e.g. about five years) of the permitted rate are recommended. Our experience has shown that the pressure on price increase was greater whenever the two electricity companies engaged in rapid capital expansion. To avoid wide fluctuations in prices, a system of graduated permitted rate of return could be adopted. Such a system would impose a lower permitted rate of return on a regulated firm at the beginning, but allow it to earn a higher permitted rate in subsequent periods (when the firm has completed its expansion scheme). It is hoped that the system would stabilize electricity prices over time.

(3) Preventing Over-Expansion

Under the existing Scheme of Control, the permitted return is entirely based on the fixed assets of the regulated company, regardless of whether the assets are "used and useful". The regulator has to exercise his own judgement to approve or disallow the expansion plan submitted by the regulated company. Once the plan has been approved, tariffs are adjusted accordingly to enable the company to earn the permitted return.

Electricity supply is a capital-intensive industry. The construction of generators and transmission networks requires huge capital investment. If the permitted rate is set too high, there will be a tendency for electricity companies to over-estimate demand growth. If the permitted rate of return is set at a level to reflect the cost of capital correctly, then over-expansion can be curtailed. However, this lowers the regulated firm's incentive to reduce costs and shifts the risk from the producers entirely over to the consumers. To prevent over-expansion, the Government should design some self-revelation mechanism to encourage truthful forecasts of demand growth. In recent years, economic literature in this area has been expanding.

(4) Introducing Competition in the Industry

In the long term, if real competition is in place in the electricity industry, then the rate-of-return regulation and price control imposed by the Government are not necessary. At present, the average price charged by HEC is higher than that of CLP. There are two suggestions to close the price differential: merging and increased competition. However, the merging of the two companies may reduce their incentives to operate efficiently, or may result in scale diseconomies. From the studies in the United States and the United Kingdom, an integrated transmission and distribution network can reduce cost substantially. Hence, a tentative approach is to put the transmission and distribution networks under a separate entity, other than CLP and HEC. If such structural separation proves to be difficult, we can maintain the existing industrial structure, but allow the two companies to share each other's networks by paying an access price. If the two private companies fail to reach agreement, the Government should act as an arbitrator in setting the access price for the use of the other company's network. In Hong Kong, a similar arrangement has been made for the three new telephone companies to use Hongkong Telephone's (HKT) network.

On the generation and supply of electricity, HEC should be allowed to compete with the associated generating companies of CLP in Hong Kong and China. As a first step, they could make long-term contracts with large users (e.g. industrial and commercial users, and also users in the same housing estates) and then plan their capacity expansion ahead. The Government could change the existing situation of regional monopoly by allowing competition in certain stages of electricity production and supply. Competition at the wholesale level and in coordination sales in the United States and the United Kingdom has been found to be feasible and has enhanced efficiency in the industry. Since the two companies' systems are interconnected via a tie line with 720 MVA capacity, this makes competition between them possible.

From the U.K. experience, competition in power generation is not workable if the market is dominated by one or two large firms. To avoid the exercise of market power by CLP under a duopolistic market structure, new entrants into the generation market should be encouraged. One possibility would be to allow the import of electricity from China. The completion of the Daya Bay nuclear power station and austerity measures in China have resulted in a surplus of electricity in certain areas in the Guangdong Province. Instead of building new generators in Hong Kong, we could make use of the surplus energy in China by encouraging private companies to import electricity. Apart from avoiding many of the environmental problems associated with power generation, this would increase the number of competitors in our electricity industry. This option is also feasible as the electricity systems in the two places are already inter-connected.

Instead of building new power plants in Hong Kong, CLP and HEC should be encouraged to purchase cheaper energy from areas within or outside Hong Kong. In this respect, the case of the United States in the 1980s is illuminating. The companies should purchase electricity from other areas if the purchase price is lower than the full avoided cost. Full avoided cost is defined as the incremental cost of generating electricity (including capacity cost) incurred by an electricity company. Such an arrangement of mandatory purchase would enhance competition, put pressure on the two electricity companies to lower costs, and close the existing tariff differential.

Under the existing Scheme of Control, the two electricity companies are obliged to promote demand-side management and energy conservation. Since the permitted return is entirely based on fixed assets, they have no incentive to promote conservation: their asset base and permitted return would be reduced if they could successfully control demand growth. Allowing competition in the electricity industry would provide an incentive for an electricity company to promote demand-side management. A firm under competition will try to adopt different pricing arrangements which can lower the prices paid by the customers. By encouraging users to shift their demands to off-peak periods, the firm can effectively reduce the costs of supplying electricity. Besides, if an electricity company can successfully introduce measures to promote energy conservation, it should be allowed to share the benefit from the cost avoided.

The restructuring of the electricity industry should involve the gas industry. Because of the slowing down in the demand growth for electricity in Hong Kong and from China, the two electricity companies, particularly CLP, are now running with substantial surplus in their generating capacities. CLP should be required to delay its expansion plan of building gas-fired generators. The natural gas saved from generating electricity could then be used for other purposes, such as gas heating and cooking. This would then put competitive pressure on the towngas company to improve efficiency.

To enhance competition in the telecommunications industry in Hong Kong, the Office of the Telecommunications Authority (OFTA) was established in July 1993. Since its inception, OFTA has taken over all the tasks previously performed by the Telecommunications Branch of the Post Office. In the electricity industry, different government departments (which include the Economic Services Branch, the Electrical and Mechanical Services Department and the Environmental Protection Department) share the responsibility of regulating the two electricity companies in Hong Kong. As the electricity system in Hong Kong expands and integrates with the system in southern China, the Government should consider whether it is necessary to set up a unified regulatory body similar to OFTA governing the electricity industry. The role of this regulatory body, if created, should be restricted to formulating coherent policies to enhance efficiency and market competition in the electricity industry.

When introducing changes into the existing system, there are inevitably some trade-offs. Increased competition in the electricity industry would eliminate cross-subsidization among different groups of users. There is also a problem of coordinating different electricity systems and ensuring system reliability. Open competition would raise a firm's business risk and the cost of capital. We have to weigh the benefit of increased efficiency against the higher cost of capital incurred.

7.3 Concluding Remarks

Although CLP and HEC's profit control schemes were extended for 15 years on largely unchanged terms, several other utilities' Schemes of Control have been heavily revised. Hongkong Telephone's (HKT) profit control scheme expired in March 1991. After lengthy negotiations, the Government reached an agreement with HKT under which profit control was removed. In June 1992, the Government announced its decision to allow other companies to provide local telephone services by 1995. The rate-of-return regulation of Hong Kong Telephone has also been replaced by the price-cap regulation (RPI-4%, for three years).

In addition, the Government announced the scrapping of the Scheme of Control with China Motor Bus (CMB) after the contract expired in 1993. The Government, dissatisfied with CMB's services, also withdrew its franchise to operate certain routes and granted this to another bus company, Citybus. As a result, CMB is no longer protected by any profit or price control scheme. Under the new franchise, CMB is not guaranteed permitted returns and has to compete with another bus company on Hong Kong Island. In 1994, the Government only allowed CMB to increase prices to earn a rate of return of 6.5% (which is much lower than the inflation rate and the cost of equity capital as measured by the CAPM), and there have been various signs to indicate that the company might give up its operations altogether in the future.[3] The Government also intends to end the Scheme of Control with Kowloon Motor Bus (KMB) before the contract expires in 1997.

Air cargo and airport luggage handling services are also provided by monopolists subject to profit control schemes. In 1992, the Provisional Airport Authority invited firms interested in providing such services at the new airport to submit letters of intent. The authority made it clear that more than one company may be licensed to provide these services. If this happens, such services will no longer be monopolized and the profit control scheme may become unnecessary.

Despite regulatory reforms in the telecommunications and transportation industries, the Government is hesitant about introducing reforms into the electricity industry. Undoubtedly, a long-term regulatory contract between a private firm and the Government, such as the Scheme of Control, could facilitate long-term capacity expansion, secure lower cost of debt financing and reduce contracting costs with suppliers. However, as evidence has shown, the Scheme fails to

---

3. On 5 October 1994, a Transport Branch spokesman mentioned that the Government was considering ways and means to strengthen the relevant legislation to better protect the interests of bus passengers. One possibility was that the Government could take over a bus company's vehicles and other assets if it failed to perform effectively.

limit price increases because returns on utilities are guaranteed and the permitted rates are not determined appropriately. In practice, consumers have paid higher prices as the actual rate of return on equity capital is higher than the cost of equity capital. In the words of one Hong Kong newspaper editorial, "a silent revolution in the regulation of public utilities in Hong Kong is taking place." (*Ming Pao*, 25 November 1992) But this revolution has yet to take place in the electricity industry. It is hoped that our studies will provide a first step to restructuring the Hong Kong electricity industry.

References

Averch, H., and L. L. Johnson. 1962. "Behaviour of the Firm under Regulatory Constraint." *American Economic Review*, Vol. 52, pp. 1052–1069.

Armstrong, Mark, S. Cowan, and J. Vickers. 1994. *Regulatory Reform: Economic Analysis and British Experience.* Cambridge: The MIT Press.

Bailey, E. E., and R. D. Coleman. 1971. "The Effect of Lagged Regulation in an Averch-Johnson Model." *Bell Journal of Economics and Management Science*, Vol. 2, pp. 278–292.

Bailey, E. E., and J. C. Malone. 1970. "Resource Allocation and the Regulated Firm." *Bell Journal of Economics and Management Science*, Vol. 1, pp. 129–142.

Baumol, W. J., and A. K. Klevorick. 1970. "Input Choices and Rate-of-return Regulation: An Overview of the Discussion." *Bell Journal of Economics and Management Science*, Vol. 2, pp. 162–190.

Beesley, Michael E. 1992. "The Required Rate of Return/Cost of Capital." In *Privatization, Regulation and Deregulation*, pp. 90–95. London: Rouledge.

Beesley, Michael E., and S. C. Littlechild. 1989. "The Regulation of Privatized Monopolies in the United Kingdom." *Rand Journal of Economics*, Vol. 20, pp. 454–472.

Berry, David. 1989. "US Cogeneration Policy in Transition." *Energy Policy* (October), pp. 471–484.

Boyes, William J. 1976. "An Empirical Examination of the Averch-Johnson Effect." *Economic Inquiry*, Vol. 17, pp. 25–35.

Braeutigam, R. R., and J. C. Panzar. 1993. "Effects of the Change from Rate-of-Return to Price-Cap Regulation." *AEA Papers and Proceedings*, Vol. 83, pp. 191–198.

British Gas Corporation International Consultancy Service

(BGCICS). 1981. *Report on the Safety and Legal Aspects of Both Town Gas and LPG Operations in Hong Kong*. Hong Kong: BGCICS.

Bruce, Alistair, and Mike Wright. 1994. "Privatizing British Coal." *Energy Policy* (January), pp. 57–67.

Cameron, Nigel. 1982. *Power: The Story of China Light*. Hong Kong: Oxford University Press.

China Light & Power Company Limited (CLP). 1946–1995. *Annual Report*. Hong Kong: CLP.

Christensen, L. R., and W. H. Greene. 1976. "Economies of Scale in U.S. Electric Power Generation." *Journal of Political Economy*, Vol. 84, pp. 655–676.

Christensen, L. R., and W. H. Greene. 1978. "An Econometric Assessment of Cost Savings from Coordination in U.S. Electric Power Generation." *Land Economics*, Vol. 54, pp. 139–153.

Clarke, Roger G. 1980. "The Effect of Fuel Adjustment Clauses on the Systematic Risk and Market Values of Electric Utilities." *Journal of Finance*, Vol. 35, pp. 347–358.

Coase, Ronald H. 1950. "The Nationalization of Electricity Supply in Great Britain." *Land Economics*, Vol. 26, pp. 1–16.

Coates, Austin. 1977. *A Mountain of Light: The Story of the Hongkong Electric Company*. London: Heineman.

Consumer Council. 1995. *Assessing Competition in the Domestic Water Heating and Cooking Fuel Market*. Hong Kong: Consumer Council.

Copeland, T. E., and J. F. Weston. 1988. *Financial Theory and Corporate Policy*, 3rd edition. Reading, Mass.: Addison-Wesley Publishing Company.

Courville, Leon. 1974. "Regulation and Efficiency in the Electric Utility Industry." *Bell Journal of Economics and Management Science*, Vol. 5, pp. 53–74.

Crew, Michael A., and P. R. Kleindorfer. 1986. "Electricity." In *The Economics of Public Utility Regulation*, edited by Michael A. Crew and P. R. Kleindorfer, pp. 169–209. London: Macmillan.

Crew, Michael A., and P. R. Kleindorfer. 1987. "Productivity Incentives and Rate-of-return Regulation.". In *Regulating Utilities in an*

Era of Deregulation, edited by Michael A. Crew, pp. 7–23. London: Macmillan.

Crew, Michael A., P. R. Kleindorfer, and D. L. Schlenger. 1987. "Governance Costs of Regulation for Water Supply." In *Regulating Utilities in an Era of Deregulation*, edited by Michael A. Crew, pp. 43–62. London: Macmillan.

Dimson, Elroy. 1979. "Risk Measurement When Shares are Subject to Infrequent Trading." *Journal of Financial Economics*, Vol. 7, pp. 197–226.

Eiteman, D. K. 1962. "Interdependency of Utility Rate-Base Types, Permitted Rate of Return, and Utility Earnings." *Journal of Finance*, Vol. 17 (March), pp. 38–52.

Elton, Edwin J., and Martin J. Gruber. 1971. "Valuation and the Cost of Capital for Regulated Industries." *Journal of Finance*, Vol. 26, pp. 661–670.

Ernst & Whinney. 1984. *Consultancy to Review the Government's Monitoring Arrangement of the Power Companies —Prepared for Government of Hong Kong*. Hong Kong: Ernst & Whinney.

Estrin, Saul, P. Grout, and S. Wadhwani. 1987. "Profit-sharing and Employee Share Ownership." *Economic Policy* (April), pp. 13–62.

Fabozzi, F. J., and J. C. Francis. 1978. "Beta as a Random Coefficient." *Journal of Financial and Quantitative Analysis* (March), pp. 101–115.

Federal Energy Regulatory Commission. 1981. *Power Pooling in the United States*. FERC-0049 (December).

Ferris, Stephen P., and Anil K. Makhija. 1987. "The Impact of Regulation on the Riskiness of Electric Utilities." *Economics Letters*, Vol. 25, pp. 79–84.

Fox-Penner, Peter S. 1990. "Cogeneration After PURPA: Energy Conservation and Industry Structure." *Journal of Law and Economics* (October), pp. 517–552.

Gilbert, R. J., and D. M. Newbery. 1994. "The Dynamic Efficiency of Regulatory Constitutions." *Rand Journal of Economics* (Winter), pp. 538–554.

Greenwald, Bruce C. 1984. "Admissible Rate Bases, Fair Rates of

Return and the Structure of Regulation." *Journal of Finance*, Vol. 35, pp. 359–368.

Hager, Patrick, Stan Perry, and Bart Jones. 1995. "The Effect of Regulatory Reform on Systematic Risk in the Marketplace: A First Look." Paper presented at the 70th Western Economic Association International Annual Conference, San Diego, 8 July 1995.

Hayashi, P. M., and J. M. Trapani. 1976. "Rate of Return Regulation and the Regulated Firm's Choice of Capital-labour Ratio: Further Empirical Evidence on the Averch-Johnson Model." *Southern Economic Journal*, Vol. 42, pp. 384–398.

Hongkong Electric Company Limited (HEC). 1955–1975. *Annual Report and Accounts*. Hong Kong: HEC.

Hongkong Electric Holdings Limited (HEC). 1976–1995. *Annual Report*. Hong Kong: HEC.

Hong Kong Government. 1946–1995. *Hong Kong 1946–Hong Kong 1995*, chapter on public utilities. Hong Kong: Hong Kong Government.

Hong Kong Government. 1982b. *The Schemes of Control*. Hong Kong: Hong Kong Government.

Hong Kong Government, Census and Statistics Department. 1967. *Hong Kong Statistics 1947–1967*. Hong Kong: Hong Kong Government.

Hong Kong Government, Census and Statistics Department. 1970–1993. *Hong Kong Monthly Statistics Digest*. Hong Kong: Hong Kong Government.

Hong Kong Government, Census and Statistics Department. 1970–1995. *Hong Kong Annual Statistics Digest*. Hong Kong: Hong Kong Government.

Hong Kong Government, Electricity Supply Companies Commission. 1959. *Electricity Supply Companies Commission — Report*. Hong Kong: Hong Kong Government.

Hong Kong Government, Finance Branch. 1994. *Review on Government Utilities*. Hong Kong: Hong Kong Government.

Hong Kong Standard. 11 December 1958.

Huettner, D. A., and J. H. Landon. 1978. "Electric Utilities: Scale

Economies and Diseconomies." *Southern Economic Journal*, Vol. 44, pp. 883–912.

Joskow, Paul L. 1974. "Inflation and Environmental Concern: Structural Change in the Process of Public Utility Price Regulation." *Journal of Law and Economics*, Vol. 16, pp. 291–327.

Joskow, Paul L. 1986. "Incentive Regulation for Electric Utilities." *Yale Journal on Regulation*, Vol. 4, pp. 1–49.

Joskow, Paul L., and Paul W. MacAvoy. 1975. "Regulation and the Financial Condition of the Electric Power Companies in the 1970's." *American Economic Review*, Vol. 65, pp. 295–301.

Joskow, Paul L., and Richard Schmalensee. 1983. *Markets for Power: An Analysis of Electric Utility Deregulation*. Cambridge: The MIT Press.

Jurewitz, John L. 1988. "Deregulation of Electricity: A View From Utility Management." *Contemporary Policy Issues*, Vol. 6, pp. 25–41.

Kafoglis, Milton Z. 1969. "Output of the Restrained Firm." *American Economic Review*, Vol. 59, pp. 583–589.

Kaln, Alfred E. 1971. *The Economics of Regulation*, Vol. 2, pp. 70–77. New York: John Wiley.

Kolbe, A. L., J. A. Read, and G. R. Hall. 1984. *The Cost of Capital: Estimating the Rate of Return for Public Utilities*. Cambridge: The MIT Press.

Lam, Pun-lee. 1992. "Struggle for Power." *Far Eastern Economic Review*, 27 February 1992, p. 26.

Lam, Pun-lee. 1996a. "Restructuring the Hong Kong Gas Industry." *Energy Policy* (forthcoming).

Lam, Pun-lee. 1996b. "Transition to Competition in Hong Kong's Local Telephone Industry." *Telecommunications Policy* (forthcoming).

Leibenstein, Harvey. "Allocative Efficiency vs. X-efficiency." *American Economic Review*, Vol. 56, pp. 392–412.

Lintner, John. 1965. "The Valuation of Risk Assets and the Selection of Risky Investment in Stock Portfolios and Capital Budgets." *Review of Economics and Statistics*, Vol. 47, pp. 13–37.

Liston, Catherine. 1993. "Price-cap versus Rate-of-return Regulation." *Journal of Regulatory Economics*, Vol. 5, pp. 25–48.

Littlechild, Stephen. 1983. *Regulation of British Telecommunications' Profitability*. London: HMSO.

Litzenberger, R., K. Ramaswamy, and H. Sosin. 1980. "On the CAPM Approach to the Estimation of a Public Utility's Cost of Equity Capital." *Journal of Finance* (May), pp. 369–383.

Liu, Pak-wai. 1990. "Utilities and Telecommunications." In *The Other Hong Kong Report 1990*, edited by Richard Y. C. Wong and Joseph Y. S. Cheng, pp. 339–353. Hong Kong: The Chinese University Press.

Liu, Pak-wai. 1991. "Utilities and Telecommunications: Regulation of Monopolies." In *The Other Hong Kong Report 1991*, edited by Sung Yun-wing and Lee Ming-kwan, pp. 259–273. Hong Kong: The Chinese University Press.

Lyon, Thomas P. 1995. "Regulatory Hindsight Review and Innovation by Electric Utilities." *Journal of Regulatory Economics*, Vol. 7, pp. 233–254.

MacAvoy, Paul W. 1970. "The Effectiveness of the Federal Power Commission." *Bell Journal of Economics and Management Science*, Vol. 1, pp. 271–303.

Mao, Elley. 1980. "The Electric Power Industry in Hong Kong: An Analysis with Special Reference to Price, Cost and Demand." M.Phil. thesis, University of Hong Kong.

Meyer, Robert A. 1976. "Capital Structure and the Behavior of the Regulated Firm under Uncertainty." *Southern Economic Journal*, Vol. 42, pp. 600–609.

Ming Pao. 14 November 1991, 25 November 1992, 2 December 1992, 1 November 1993.

Mossin, Jan. 1966. "Equilibrium in a Capital Asset Market." *Econometrica*, Vol. 34, pp. 768–783.

Mueller, Milton. 1991. *International Telecommunications in Hong Kong*. Hong Kong: The Chinese University Press.

Murphy, F. H., and A. L. Soyster. 1983. *Economic Behaviour of Electric Utilities*. New Jersey: Prentice-Hall.

Nelson, R. A., and W. J. Primeaux. 1984. "Rate Base Valuation

Procedures and the Behaviour of Regulated Firms." *Quarterly Review of Economics and Business*, Vol. 24 (Winter), pp. 72–81.

Norton, Seth W. 1985. "Regulation and Systematic Risk: The Case of Electric Utilities." *Journal of Law and Economics*, Vol. 28, pp. 671–686.

Nowotny, Kenneth, and James Peach. 1992. "Changes in Energy Consumption, 1970–1989, and Energy Policy in the United States." *Journal of Economic Issues*, Vol. 26, pp. 183–196.

Pak, S. L. 1983. "Public Utilities in Hong Kong: A Study of Returns on Investments to the Company and to the Shareholders." M.Phil. thesis, University of Hong Kong.

Petersen, H. Craig. 1975. "An Empirical Test of Regulatory Effects." *Bell Journal of Economics*, Vol. 6, pp. 111–126.

Priest, George L. 1993. "The Origins of Utility Regulation and the 'Theories of Regulation' Debate." *Journal of Law and Economics* (April), pp. 289–323.

Primeaux, W. J. 1978. "Rate Base Methods and Realized Rates of Return." *Economic Inquiry*, Vol. 16 (January), pp. 95–107.

Roberts, Jane, David Elliott, and Trevor Houghton. 1991. *Privatizing Electricity: the Politics of Power*. London and New York: Belhaven Press.

Robison, H. David, Wallace N. Davidson III, and John L. Glascock. 1995. "The Formation of Public Utility Holding Companies and Their Subsequent Diversification Activity." *Journal of Regulatory Economics*, Vol. 7, pp. 199–214.

Sharpe, W. F. 1963. "A Simplified Model for Portfolio Analysis." *Management Science*, Vol. 9, pp. 277–293.

Sharpe, W. F. 1964. "Capital Asset Prices: A Theory of Market Equilibrium under Conditions of Risk." *Journal of Finance*, Vol. 19, pp. 425–442.

Spanne, Robert M. 1974. "Rate of Return Regulation and Efficiency in Production: An Empirical Test of the Averch-Johnson Thesis." *Bell Journal of Economics and Management Science*, Vol. 5, pp. 38–53.

Spiegel, Yossef, and Daniel F. Spulber. 1994. "The Capital Structure of a Regulated Firm." *Rand Journal of Economics*, Vol. 25, pp. 424–440.

Steiner, P. O. 1957. "Peak Loads and Efficient Pricing." *Quarterly Journal of Economics*, Vol. 71, pp. 585–610.

Summerton, Janes, and Ted K. Bradshaw. 1991. "Towards a Dispersed Electrical System: Challenges to the Grid." *Energy Policy* (January/February), pp. 24–34.

Takayama, Akira. 1969. "Behaviour of the Firm under Regulatory Constraint." *American Economic Review*, Vol. 59, pp. 255–260.

Vickers, John, and George Yarrow. 1988. "The Energy Industries." In *Privatization: An Economic Analysis*, pp. 243–340. Cambridge: The MIT Press.

Vickers, John, and George Yarrow. 1991a. "The British Electricity Experiment." *Economic Policy: An European Forum*, Vol. 12, pp. 188–231.

Vickers, John, and George Yarrow. 1991b. "Economic Perspectives on Privatization." *Journal of Economic Perspectives*, Vol. 5, pp. 111–132.

Vickrey, William. 1971. "Responsive Pricing of Public Utility Services." *Bell Journal of Economics and Management Science*, Vol. 2, pp. 337–346.

Vickrey, William. 1987. "Marginal and Average Cost Pricing." In *The New Palgrave: A Dictionary of Economics*, pp. 311–317. London: Macmillan.

Vogelsang, I., and J. Finsinger. 1979. "A Regulatory Adjustment Process for Optimal Pricing by Multiproduct Monopoly Firms." *Bell Journal of Economics*, Vol. 10, pp. 157–171.

Water Services Association (UK), and Water Companies Association. 1991. *The Cost of Capital in the Water Industry*, Vols. 1–3. London: Water Services Association.

Waterson, Michael. 1990. "The Major Utilities: Ownership, Regulation and Energy Usage." In *A New Economic Policy for Britain: Essays on the Development of Industry*, edited by Keith Cowling and Roger Sugden, pp. 174–191. Manchester and New York: Manchester University Press.

Wellisz, Stanislaw H. 1963. "Regulation of Natural Gas Pipeline

Companies: An Economic Analysis." *Journal of Political Economy*, Vol. 71, pp. 30–43.

Weyman-Jones, Thomas G. 1990. "RPI-X Price Cap Regulation: The Price Controls Used in UK Electricity." *Utilities Policy*, pp. 65–77.

Yarrow, George. 1986. "Regulation and Competition in the Electricity Supply Industry." In *Privatization & Regulation — the UK Experience*, edited by John Kay, Colin Mayer, and David Thompson, pp. 189–209. Oxford: Clarendon Press.

Yarrow, George. 1994. "Privatization, Restructuring, and Regulatory Reform in Electricity Supply." In *Privatization & Economic Performance*, edited by Matthew Bishop, John Kay, and Colin Mayer, pp. 62–88. Oxford: Oxford University Press.

Zajac, Edward E. 1970. "A Geometric Treatment of Averch-Johnson's Behaviour of the Firm Model." *American Economic Review*, Vol. 60, pp. 117–125.

Index

Already Published

《開放的航空業》
　　鄺啓新著、鄧文正譯

《市場環保主義：香港的借鏡》
　　鄺美慈著、鄧文正譯

《中國經濟改革：分析、反省、前瞻》
　　徐滇慶、雷鼎鳴、張欣合編

《佛利民在中國》
　　米爾頓・佛利民著、鄧文正譯

《香港醫療服務的經濟分析》
　　許早洱著

《規劃條例及都市經濟運作》
　　森姆・史泰利著

《中國的奇蹟：發展戰略與經濟改革》
　　林毅夫、蔡昉、李周著

《國體與經體：對阿當・斯密夫原理的一種詮釋》
　　Joseph Cropsey著、鄧文正譯

《獨共南山守中國》
　　胡國亨著